STRATEGY
WITH
PASSION:

A LEADER'S GUIDE TO
EXPLOITING THE FUTURE

Christine A.R. MacNulty, FRSA
Stephen R. Woodall, Ph.D.

What Others Are Saying About
Strategy with Passion

"Christine and Steve have joined forces to develop a method for understanding people in ways that are complementary to the values we cherish and is revolutionary in its approach to strategic planning. I firmly believe this new combined approach is superior to anything else available anywhere, and It can assist military operations, the intelligence community and even policy makers. It is a must read and can be used for any country or culture anywhere in the world.
...a great read by the way!"

LTG (R) Mike Flynn, Former Director, Defense Intelligence Agency.

"Today's most successful business leaders are "ninja innovators," who embrace adaptability, decisiveness and a mission-oriented strategy. *Strategy with Passion: A Leader's Guide to Exploiting the Future* recognizes that great leaders must be open to change. Success requires not only evaluating opportunities and threats, but innovative, visionary and passionate leaders who keep their businesses evolving. Christine MacNulty and Stephen Woodall show why leaders must own the strategic planning process."

Gary Shapiro, President & CEO, Consumer Technology Association

"Passion leads reason in action. Reason is the work of our minds. If we could, we recall all a priori and a posteriori knowledge to act. Passion, is the work of our hearts. It is a force multiplier. "Passion" becomes the "Reason" when we know in our hearts "WHY" we need to get there. Shared enthusiasm demands seeing a shared future. Chris and Steve are the alchemists. They unveil the perfect recipe in "strategy with passion". A must read for the exceptional leader. A compass for getting THERE."

The Honorable Bijan R. Kian, Member, Board of Directors
Export-Import Bank of the United States (2006-2011),

"In days when businesses are dominated by specialized units, MacNulty and Woodall highlight the importance of a strategic vision to drive and direct growth and to inspire the executive and work force. They lay out a workshop technique to generate this vision and to create stakeholders in its realization and execution. An important contribution to corporate transformation thinking"

Dr. Jon Glassman, Ambassador (ret), former Director for Government Policy, Northrop Grumman Electronic Systems

"Few leaders today really understand strategy – what it is, why it requires creativity, analysis and synthesis, and how to develop an effective strategic plan. Even fewer know how to implement one. Chris and Steve have been helping leaders develop and implement vision-based strategic plans for more than 25 years, and in this book they have shared their 11-step process and many humorous anecdotes."

Dr. Lani Kass, Corporate Strategic Advisor and Senior Vice President, CACI International , Former Senior Policy Advisor to the Chairman of the Joint Chiefs of Staff (CJCS)

Publisher: Triumph World Press, Fairfax Station, VA, 22039
Cover Design: Kathi Dunn, www.dunn-design.com
Interior Design: Jim Bisakowski, Book Design
Editing: Marla Markman

ISBN: 978-0-9909286-4-5 (paper)
ISBN: 978-0-9909286-3-8 (mobi - kindle)
ISBN: 978-0-9909286-5-2 (epub)

MacNulty, Christine A. Ralph, author.
        Strategy with passion : a leader's guide to
        exploiting the future / Christine A.R. MacNulty, Stephen
        R. Woodall.
          pages cm
          Includes index.
          ISBN 978-0-9909286-4-5
          ISBN 978-0-9909286-3-8
          ISBN 978-0-9909286-5-2

        1. Strategic planning. 2. Business planning.
        3. Management. 4. Leadership.   I. Woodall, Stephen R.,
        author. II. Title.

        HD30.28.M284 2016   658.4'012
                        QBI16-900013

Books may be purchased in quantity and/or special sales by contacting the authors at info@strategywithpassion.com.

CONTENTS

Dedication

We dedicate this book to our spouses, Kirk and Nancy, for their patience and support during the writing of our book. Special thanks to Kirk for his willingness to edit a succession of draft versions.

Acknowledgements

The authors want to acknowledge, with deep appreciation, their friends, colleagues, and clients who have shared their perspectives, planning tools, and experiences in the course of their many years of consultancy.

In particular, we would like to thank Les Higgins, who has been part of our team since its inception. Les, originally an electronics engineer-turned-social-change-consultant, has helped with the design and execution of many of our workshops, and has provided much valuable insight. We would also like to thank Elizabeth Allingham, our team psychologist, who made a significant contribution to the psychological component of our workshops. Prior to Elizabeth joining the team, John Powderly provided our initial understanding of group dynamics and processes.

Finally, we would like to thank our many clients who have provided us with interesting, meaningful, and fun projects. Three, especially, come to mind: Pat Tracey, John Hanley and the late Tim Holden, who have remained friends since we first met.

Foreword

Choosing to engage in strategic planning activities is an act of ulti-
mate optimism, reflecting a leader's conviction that an advantageous
future can evolve. Strategic planning approached through the lens of
the Vision-Based Planning framework Christine MacNulty and Steve
Woodall have developed is about more than that. It is about the leadership of an enterprise discovering a shared concept of what matters to
them about the future and who and what they must become *together* to
achieve it.

Chris is a mathematician who has an engineer's curiosity for how
humans and human systems behave as well as a gift for explaining complex enterprises using simplified concepts. Steve was, and *is,* by nature
one of the "mavericks" referred to in the book—a constant fount of new
and unusual ideas. Together, they have developed a process that runs
from mind-expanding and highly visionary to pragmatic and highly
actionable. And they make it fun.

Although I was privileged to meet Chris and Steve earlier in my
career, my opportunity to experience their workshops came when I took
responsibility for a large and complex organization whose leadership
believed they had been discarded by the enterprise they had devoted
their lives to. Huge changes were happening in the environment around
us, dramatically increasing the importance and challenge of our mission. Maintaining the status quo would threaten the future capability of
the entire enterprise, but the leadership team doubted that real change
was within their grasp. The Vision-Based Planning workshops Chris
and Steve led reignited the passion of our team for the institution we
loved. The vision and plans we coalesced reflected our deeply shared
sense of responsibility for ensuring the readiness of the next generation.
As much as the inspiration of our vision, the specificity of our action
plans secured an unprecedented level of investment to effect change.

We accomplished many things together during my tenure, and when the vision and plans were revisited three years after my departure, they formed the basis of an even larger and more ambitious campaign.

Strategy with Passion is exactly what Chris and Steve do. And it is contagious.

VADM Pat Tracey, USN (Ret)

Vice President, Homeland Security and Defense,

HP Enterprise Services

Introduction

Why We Wrote this Book— and What Makes It Different

Strategic planning should be easy and fun. After all, you're developing the description of how to achieve the wonderful, creative vision that you have of your organization. Yet so many leaders and their teams struggle with it, complaining that it takes too much time and effort, or that the strategic planning consultants they have brought in to do their planning for them don't understand their business, or are taking too long and costing too much. It shouldn't be that way. Others question the validity of planning in these turbulent, fast-paced times, saying that if we can't predict (which is generally true), then how can we plan?

We are passionate in our belief that strategy and planning are still the two most critical elements of an organization's success, and we anticipate that our own perspectives and understanding will ignite the same passion in others—you, for instance. We want to show you that the planning process can be one of the most rewarding activities you can undertake, both intellectually and financially.

While books on strategy and strategic planning abound, this one sets out a method which, if followed, can provide you with a successful strategic plan quickly and easily, and which enables you to easily update the plan. This book is also designed to cut through some of the jargon and fads that surround strategic planning, and introduce a clear and passionate vision for the value of strategic planning.

The title of our book contains two ideas not normally associated with strategy and strategic planning: *passion* and *exploiting the future.*

Most people regard strategic planning as an intellectual exercise that must be done, yet rarely offers any significant insights and takes time away from the important operations of the day, as we have already mentioned. Many leaders also view it as a function that can be passed off to a staff group or consultants who prepare a report called a strategic plan.

If either of these is your view, you are missing out on one of the most rewarding and beneficial opportunities as a leader. A strategic plan should be visionary and inspiring. It should fire up you and everyone in your organization with passion and enthusiasm.

If it does not ignite passion and enthusiasm, then it is not doing its job. *Nothing great was ever achieved without enthusiasm.* —Emerson

Exploiting the future is another powerful concept we will demonstrate. Too often we hear leaders discussing the future as if it were inevitable; as if organizations must expect to be battered about by circumstances; as if they have no power over their own future.

Most organizations have much more ability to determine their own future than they realize. It just takes some effort to see themselves and their strategic environment differently, and then be willing to change— to trim their sails as necessary.

Photo © Dan Nerney/NYYC

One ship sails East,

And another West,

By the self-same winds that blow,

'Tis the set of their sails

And not the gales

That tells the way we go

       —Ella Wheeler Wilcox

Most people accept that start-ups—especially businesses started in their garages by young, enthusiastic people—have visions that inspire their owners, but by the time an organization is extremely large and mature, the sparkle of that vision has generally disappeared. By the time the business is several decades and leaders away from its founder, the leader is frequently bound to the *status quo* and strategies become budget-driven. No organization has ever succeeded with a budget-driven strategy. We need only look at the Department of Defense to see how well that works. But this tired, mature organization need not necessarily be that way. It's possible to see its future through new eyes, from a new perspective, and to see the potential that could be there—especially when leadership incorporates creativity and intuition into its planning process.

Time spent thinking creatively about their organization not only gives leadership greater belief in their ability to determine their own future, but it also shortens the time spent weighing the pros and cons, and thinking about all that can go wrong. In fact, our complete Vision-Based Planning process takes approximately one-fourth the time of a more traditional strategic planning method, yet produces greater success.

Both of us believe strongly and passionately in the value of strategy, strategic thinking, and planning. We have seen the joy our clients have had in developing their visions and strategic plans, their commitment to them, and the way the process has enabled them to handle unexpected circumstances and problems. We would like leaders, from any type and size of organization, to realize that their enterprises can be fun, rewarding, and successful if they approach their planning with the right mind-set.

Although the focus of this book is organizational strategic planning, the same processes can be applied to R&D planning, marketing planning and new business development. Another area in which our Vision-Based Planning has had remarkable success is for new organizations emerging from an acquisition or merger, a move that requires significant cultural change.

How to Use this Book

Strategy with Passion explains the rationale behind our approach and why an organization should plan this way. It also covers all the steps in our Vision-Based Planning process and details the techniques that can be used during the process.

The book is based on first-hand experiences using Vision-Based Planning with our clients. However, you do not need to attend one of our workshops to reap the benefits of this approach. Anyone can take these techniques and processes and use them as we describe. In this case, *Strategy with Passion* would be used as a guidebook for our 11-step Vision-Based Planning process.

Following this Introduction and Chapter 1, the book is divided into four parts and should be read in chapter order, since each chapter builds on the knowledge of the previous one.

Chapter 1 describes some early experiences in our work together that provided insights into those misperceptions and that gave us an entirely different perspective on planning.

STRATEGY WITH PASSION

Part I: Pre-Planning Considerations and Requirements

Chapter 2 sets the scene for the planning process—explaining what strategy and planning are all about, and providing definitions of Vision, Mission, Values and more.

Chapter 3 covers the importance of effective leadership, and discusses what that means.

Part II: Preparation for the Workshops

Chapter 4 covers the things that need to be done to understand thoroughly the context and environment within which the organization operates.

Chapter 5 describes how to turn information about the external operating environment into useful, actionable intelligence.

Chapter 6 gives detailed descriptions about how much time to allow for workshop sessions and how to organize for both plenary and small group sessions.

Part III: The Vision-Based Planning Process

Chapter 7 provides an introduction to our Vision-Based Planning process and the kinds of techniques and methods we use.

Chapter 8 describes Phase 1—the critically important Expansionary and Exploratory phase of our process where the real creative thinking takes place.

Chapter 9 provides detailed descriptions and examples of many of the tools and techniques we use during Phase 1, including purpose and order.

Chapter 10 describes Phase 2—the synthesis of all the material from Phase 1 into the entire Vision-Based strategic plan, including Vision, Mission, Values, Top-Level Goals, Objectives, Action and Implementation Plan.

Part IV: What's Next?

Chapter 11 discusses the importance of a plan to communicate the new Vision-Based Strategic Plan to all the major stakeholders, both internal and external, and provides details of how to develop it.

Chapter 12 covers the importance of cultural change when implementing a new Vision and Vision-Based Strategic Plan, and shows how our VBP process can assist with the cultural change.

Chapter 13 is about what to do to implement the Vision-Based Strategy, how a small Strategic Planning Group can help, and how to update the Vision and Plan in the light of significant changes in either the internal organizational structure, or major changes in the external environment.

Glossary: This provides definitions of some of the words and terms we use, since we have found that there are multiple, differing definitions of many of them.

Appendices

Appendix 1: Social Value Groups provides a description of a values-based model that we use for understanding people, whether they are employees, customers, or other stakeholders.

Appendix 2: Nth Order Effects covers the importance of understanding strategy from a system's perspective and the kinds of unanticipated consequences of not thinking through this way. It provides an example of some disastrous Nth order effects

Look for our *Sheeple* People in each Chapter

We hope you enjoy our illustrations featuring Steve's cartoon "Sheeples" in action—reflecting the subject matter—at the beginning of each chapter!

CHAPTER 1

Experiences That Shaped Our Approach

Where the Passion Came From

Both of us had been involved in developing strategy and strategic plans for large complex organizations when we came together in 1994 at the suggestion of a mutual friend and colleague who told us that we thought alike. Chris had been a futurist and technology forecaster early in her career, while Steve was a naval officer who had command experience and had worked in strategy in the Pentagon. We did not have conventional management consultancy experience, so we were not bound by any particular consultancy's methods or models. We both had mathematical backgrounds, we both thought strategically, we could be both serious and logical, yet we both had a quirky side—driving fast cars fast, enjoying science fiction and other out-of-the-box thinking, and having fun. When we started on our joint consulting work, we hadn't thought about incorporating this lighter side in our work, but it occurred with one particular client, and when it happened, we realized that it could be of great benefit to our clients and their strategies. We called this an experience of both head and heart.

Head and Heart

In 1995 and 1996, we worked with a remarkable client: Naval Special Warfare Group ONE (Navy SEALs). We have not seen such passionate people before or since. They were brilliant, funny, loyal, absolutely dedicated to what they were doing, and incredibly courageous. In the course of our work with them, they introduced innovations into their organizational structure and technology-based systems, transforming an organization that was seen as tactical and unconventional into a strategic asset for the country.

We wondered what it was the SEALs were doing (or being) that led to such success. It seemed to be a combination of brains and passion—head and heart.

The emphasis in many organizations, both commercial and in the defense/government sector, is on science and technology. Those two areas have provided our nation with amazing and beneficial products and services. They have enabled us to become and remain world leaders economically, technologically, and strategically. But technology alone could not, and cannot, achieve that. People, processes, and organizations are also required, yet little emphasis has been placed on those needs, especially on the people aspects.

People and relationships are fuzzier and less easy to control than technologies and processes. However, the softer, people aspects of good leadership and management are now supported by neuroscience, as well as by psychology. This may increase the willingness of scientifically-based leaders and managers to take the people requirement more seriously.

If we are to achieve the focus and direction that will make us successful in industry, commerce, defense, and world politics, then we must ensure that we pay attention to two areas: the head and the heart.

The *head* covers all capabilities that involve knowledge, thinking, reasoning, analysis, objectivism, positivism, and reductionism. These capabilities—we call them strategic thinking capabilities—provide focus.

STRATEGY WITH PASSION

The *heart* includes all capabilities that involve understanding, synthesis, creativity, passion, imagination, inspiration, and intuition. These capabilities—that are the core of our Vision-Based Planning (VBP)—are essential for direction and power.

Effective decision-making requires both. Figure 1.1 indicates the relationships and feedback between the head and heart processes, and in our VBP method, we cycle between them.

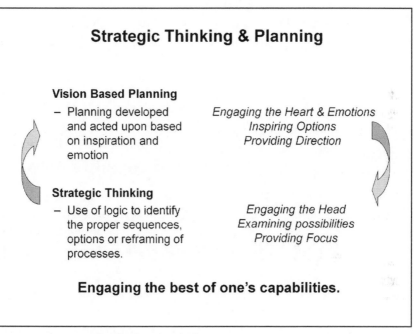

Figure 1-1: *Strategic Thinking and Planning*

The "Aha!" Moment

It was 2 am when our team awakened to the sound of hammering on doors and feet running down the corridor. It was our second night at the SEALs' new training center on San Clemente Island, and we had already accomplished two very intensive days of strategic planning workshops. Because the SEALs like to get plenty of exercise, we started each day early and finished about 6:30 pm. Then our team prepared for the following day, while the SEALs drank beer and continued to discuss the subjects that the workshop had raised. On this night, our team had gone to bed before the SEALs.

No one knocked on our doors that night. It seemed that one of the SEALs was shouting to his buddies to get up and go to the conference room because he'd just had a great idea. A few minutes later, the sleeping quarters were in silence as all the SEALs had left. Over breakfast, we asked the SEALs what had happened. It turned out that one of them had awakened with such a good idea related to their strategic planning project, that he couldn't wait until morning to share it. Except for a bit of friendly joshing, all the SEALs had gone to join their enthusiastic buddy without any complaints.

Later that day we were working on developing the vision for the SEALs. A vision is a very important part of a strategic plan, and we work hard at getting it exactly right. The SEALs had been working in small groups and, as we went back to the plenary session, we saw that one of the participants was missing. His colleagues assured us that he would be back very soon.

It is worth mentioning that the dress for these workshops was very casual—jeans or shorts, t-shirts, and flip-flops. Several minutes went by and finally the missing SEAL returned—freshly showered, and in a perfectly pressed uniform. He came into the conference room, saluted the commodore, stood to attention, and recited the vision that his small group had produced. It brought tears to our eyes. It was passionate, inspiring, and carried with it the seeds that would transform what the SEALs were doing and how they did it.

In most military organizations, where the command turns over every two years, there is frequently very little continuity. But because the SEALs who attended our workshops at the beginning and end of this particular commodore's tour became subsequent leaders and were passionate about the vision and strategic plan they developed, it remained virtually unchanged for 14 years.

We had always stressed to our clients that visions need an element of feeling or emotion, but at that moment, we saw how powerful a vision with passion could be. We had seen that kind of passion before from various business leaders. Some of those organizations succeeded brilliantly, while others worked well but not so spectacularly. We came to the conclusion that success cannot be achieved when just fueled by passion or only by a vision and strategy. It is the combination of the two that enable organizations to take off.

We learned a lot from the SEALs, and the experience caused us to think more deeply about what we were doing for our clients. Most of our team had been strategic planning consultants for more than 25 years. We had been very successful with helping our clients develop good strategic plans and, to us, strategic planning was just good common sense. But so many wonderful ideas were expressed and shared during that project and a subsequent one, and so many good things came from those workshops, according to the commodore, that we began to see strategic planning differently.

In fact, we had had an inkling of these ideas more than a decade earlier, when consulting with a major British retailer. The organization was doing rather poorly, and the leadership didn't understand why. It turned out that they had defined themselves in terms of their competitors, rather than thinking about their own vision of their business. We remember drawing a diagram of the way we perceived their business—it had many facets all facing outward, with each facet representing a competitor. In many cases, the company was competing solely on price. In the center of the diagram was a void. When we asked them what should be in the void, none of the leadership team had an answer.

We were holding our strategic planning workshops at a huge mansion that belonged to the company, and in the entrance hall was a bust of the founder. At one point in the proceedings, we asked the leadership about the history of the company—who was the founder and what was his vision? This seemed to finally elicit some animation, so we led the questions into the area of "If the founder were alive today, what would he want to do?" "What would his vision be today?" Without exception, the entire group had a real "Aha!" experience.

It became clear that the founder's vision was still relevant—although the way in which it would need to manifest was different. Everyone became passionate about this new approach to thinking about their business. The new, vision-based strategic plan that they developed was very successful. It was the "Aha!" moment of thinking about the founder, and the passion that followed that turned the business around.

Art versus Science

In the Armed Forces, there are the concepts of the Art of War and the Science of War. Generally speaking, the Science of War is concerned with platforms (ships, aircraft, etc.), combat systems, weapon systems, and all forms of information and communications technologies, while the Art of War is focused on what needs to be done to achieve our geo-political goals, win the conflict, and overcome or influence adversaries. Quite a number of senior officers in the Armed Forces are becoming concerned that, in our emphasis on the science and technology of war, we are losing our knowledge and understanding of the Art of War.

The same situation is occurring in business. We are placing too much emphasis on improving processes—making them leaner and more efficient—through the use of the latest computers, software, and information technology. We are also placing too much emphasis on growth and shareholder equity. The result is that we are losing track of the businesses we are in and the customers we are serving. Good, successful, business has always been about providing value to your customers. However, there is hope of recovery—the concept is re-emerging, as this quotation from *Forbes.com* indicates:

> Now is the time to demonstrate to a skeptical world
> the truth, goodness, and heroism of capitalism rather
> than perpetuate the false stigmas of selfishness, greed,
> and profit maximization," said (John)Mackey, citing

not only his personal experience with Whole Foods Market but also other "conscious" corporations from Google and Starbucks to Nordstrom, Patagonia, and The Container Store.

This view is endorsed by luminaries such as Paul Polman, the CEO of Anglo-Dutch consumer giant Unilever, who says that business has to learn to be successful while contributing to society and supporting eco-systems and biodiversity: "We do not have to win at the expense of others to be successful . . . winning alone is not enough, it is about winning with purpose."

The overwhelming trend is that the traditional Four Ps of sales success—price, product, place, and promotion—is being joined by a fifth essential, the new P for purpose.

While a few people can get excited and passionate about processes, technology, and finance, they are not subjects of great appeal to most people. Most people—especially young people—want to feel they are being useful, helpful, and contributing to something worthwhile. That's why this new "P"—purpose—is so important. That's what inspires people to give their best. That's what makes them passionate. Indeed, we would like to add a sixth P—passion. In the end, that's what makes an organization of any kind—military or commercial—successful.

Key Points from this Chapter

- There is much more to strategy than thinking and logic.
- Strategy is about people—the way they make decisions, the way they react or respond to events and circumstances and, above all, to what they want their organizations and themselves to be and do in the future.
- Strategists seize the future—they see what they want it to be, and reach out and grab it.

- Effective strategic planning requires a combination of head and heart. The head provides the logic, strategic thinking, and assessment of scenarios or options to providing the focus. Engaging the heart – emotion, passion and intuition – provides power, inspiring options and direction.

- Organizations that use the head and heart are more resilient, better able to cope with change, and frequently much more powerful than those run by more cautious "bean counters."

PART I:
Pre-Planning Considerations and Requirements

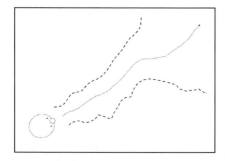

CHAPTER 2

Setting the Scene— to Exploit the Future

Why Think About The Future?

It is very difficult to know what the future will hold. As we watch or read the news each day, we see the world around us filled with dramatic surprises and turns of events that seem certain to change the trajectory of our nation and thus, to some extent, our lives.

This is all the more reason to think about your future and the future of your organization. It is particularly important, if you are a leader in your organization. As a leader, one of your duties and responsibilities is to guide your organization into the future—to plan, strategically, where you want to take it. This is especially vital if your organization is a large, complex one, with many elements competing for resources from a finite pot. Ideally, you'll need a process to follow. You and your leadership team need to reach a consensus on what your organization is for—its purpose, and perhaps also its mission—if your organization has a primarily operational purpose. You need to create a vision, shared by your leadership team that answers the question: What do you want your organization to be, or become, in the future?

There is much more to planning than extrapolating past trends and budgeting for the next year or two. Change is occurring all the time—both externally and internally to the organization—and successful businesses are those that have learned to thrive on change. Thriving on change means being aware of what is going on in the external environment from major global, political, and economic events, to what's happening to your customers, competitors, and suppliers. Understanding the context and setting the scene for future activity is all part of planning. It means anticipating change and being ready for it. And it also means "seizing the day" and taking decisions and calculated risks. Successful organizations do more than cope with change or adapt to it—they exploit it.

Clarification of Critical Terms

- *Strategic Planning* is a process of deciding where an organization wants to be at some time in the future and then producing a plan for getting there. Strategic Planning should be an ongoing process, although every few years (two to five on average) the plan should be updated during a major planning event.

- A *Strategic Plan* is the documented output from the Strategic Planning Process. It should include a Vision, Mission, Purpose, Values, Goals, Objectives, Strategies, Action Plan, and Implementation Plan. In other words, it is a specific program for achieving the Vision and Mission/Purpose. It is generally regarded as fixed – at least for a specific time – although we recommend that it be evaluated and updated through the strategic planning process.

- A *Strategy* is an overall blueprint or design for achieving a specific goal.

Once you have accomplished these things—described as a purpose/mission and a vision—you can begin to decide how to commit your resources and actions in a way that will move your organization toward the goals that will enable your vision to be realized. There is a Japanese proverb that describes the need for both vision and action.

Vision without Action is a Daydream
Action without Vision is a Nightmare

As a leader, if you do not think about the future, you are more likely to make less effective decisions, making your goals more difficult to achieve. To the extent that you do think about the future, and take what you can project and forecast into consideration, you are more likely to make better decisions that increase the likelihood that your goals will be achieved and your vision realized.

A Few Words on Forecasting, Futures and Foresight

Most competent organizations plan, to some extent, for the future—evaluating both opportunities and potential threats. It is at best, even for small organizations, an uncertain and difficult process. To be practical, plans must combine sufficient specificity and clarity to guide future actions, while retaining flexibility and robustness sufficient to allow adjustment or compensation for unforeseen circumstances. Plans must also be credible enough to be accepted by those who must put them into effect, whether they are based on a forecast or projection, or a range of possible future scenarios In the private sector, they must also be sufficiently credible to be accepted by investors.

In spite of very real problems with long-range planning and forecasting, there is enormous value in thinking about possible trends and events, and combining them into multiple scenarios; thinking through possible courses of action and attempting to identify potential negative effects. The process of doing all this can stimulate new ideas and solutions, and certainly prepares the leadership for change, as well as making them more flexible in their thinking.

To the extent that the future can be projected and the range of possibilities understood, opportunities arise in planning and policymaking decisions to foster a less adverse future than that which might occur without benefit of such preparatory and exploratory analysis.

Clarification of Critical Terms

Remember not to confuse a forecast with your strategic plan.

- A *forecast* is an assessment of specific elements of the future with some degree of confidence, by either quantitative or qualitative methods.

- A *projection* is the extension into the future of past historical trends, by some systematic method.

- A *prediction* is a statement of fact before the event occurs. This is usually difficult to do reliably.

- *Futures research* is the systematic study of possible and probable future trends, events and scenarios in order to provide insight for planning and decision-making.

- *Foresight* is sometimes used interchangeably with Futures, but it is generally more comprehensive, and includes critical and systemic thinking.

- *Prophecy* is prediction by divine inspiration, and we do not have techniques for this!

Remember that most of us mortal souls are not prophets. Steer clear of anyone who claims to be really good at predictions or prophecy!

Strategic Planning for Complex Organizations

We've said that developing strategic plans is critical for any organization, but it is especially vital for large, complex ones.

Attributes of a typical complex organization include:

- Many people, with one or more cultures.

- Many organizational elements, which can either work together or separately, or some of both.

- An organizational framework, generally a hierarchy or series of hierarchies, or matrix structures, although this may not be the case in organizations that have many merged or acquired parts.

- A system of common strategies, rules, and processes for operating and decision-making (for example, government organizations). But this is not always the case for large organizations that operate globally and have many merged or acquired parts.

Examples of complex organizations include very large, general hospitals; large city governments such as New York or Los Angeles; large universities; the Red Cross; the State Department; General Electric; Airbus Industries; Royal Dutch Shell, or the U.S. Navy.

As you can imagine, each of these organizations has very different characteristics. The one characteristic that is the most difficult to include in a strategic planning process, yet which is critically important, is culture.

Understanding Organizational Culture

Understanding the nature and attributes of the organizational culture, or cultures, in which a complex organization operates is critical.

Organizational culture is the synthesis of the values, customs, traditions, and agreed-upon meanings of words and terms that make the organization unique—and, equally important, it is also composed of people with their individual values, individual beliefs, and motivations. It is often thought of as the character of the organization, since it usually embodies the purpose and vision as set forth by the organization's founders. The values in the culture of a complex organization have a direct influence on its ethical standards, and thus can signal the expectations for the behavior of leaders and managers.

Understanding the elements of an organization's culture is especially important for strategic planning, which may require cultural changes, or the merging of two or more organizations where the cultures may differ.

The path to cultural change or the merging of different cultures requires development of a true consensus, especially on organizational values. This, in turn, provides the foundation for reaching consensus on a shared vision for the future of the organization. This subject is discussed in more detail in Chapter 11.

Reaching Consensus, Not Just Compromise

The distinction between consensus and compromise is critical, especially when working to achieve a common culture in a complex organization. When compromise is the basis for merging cultures, people in each culture have to give up something of fundamental importance to reach the compromise (from *compromissum, meaning consent reached by mutual concessions*). Compromise is a recipe for continual conflict and strife within the organization, and is often characterized by disagreements over the meaning of words or over small decisions such as who gets which parking space. In other words, expected behaviors will be less predictable.

Consensus in an organization (from *cōnsentiō,* meaning *feel together,* or *agreement*) builds a foundation for development of truly shared values and makes possible the development of a truly shared vision.

Vision, Mission, and Corporate Values

We mention these strategic plan elements here as they are critical precursors to the plan. Indeed, we cannot conceive of developing a stra-

STRATEGY WITH PASSION

tegic plan without them, yet there is often little understanding of what they are and why they are important. We take considerable time during major strategic planning events to ensure that there is consensus on all of them.

- A *Vision* is what an organization will be or become. It is generally written using existential verbs, and it describes a future state of the organization that acts as a guiding star.

- A *Mission (or Purpose)* is what the organization is for or does. It is generally written using action verbs, and it describes the motivation or reason for the organization's existence.

- *Values* are deeply held beliefs that have a strong emotional component. They create a basis for the organization's culture, and they must be shared and lived to some degree, at least, by the leadership, management and workforce.

Together these three components form the "heart and soul" of an organization, providing the context within which strategies can be developed.

Key Points from this Chapter

- There is much more to planning than extrapolating past trends and budgeting for the next year or two.

- Since many people are not aware of the breadth and depth of a good, effective strategic plan, we have laid out some guidelines and definitions, including the differences between planning and forecasting.

- It is important to understand the context within which the organization operates so that the planning can be based on the whole picture, not just a narrow, organizational perspective.

- Planning must take into account the organization's culture and values.

- It should be arrived at through a true consensus, not compromise.

- It should be developed by the leadership, not a staff group of middle managers who do not have access to all the information in the leaders' heads.

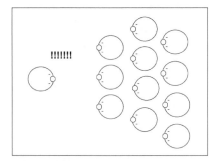

CHAPTER 3

The Importance of Effective Leadership

What is Good Leadership?

In the broadest sense of the word, "leadership" is the ability to bring people together and guide them toward a common goal. Throughout history, much has been written about what it means to be a leader. Chinese military general and *Art of War* author Sun Tzu described a leader as one who "cultivates the moral law, and strictly adheres to proper methods and discipline." Jack Welch, former chairman and CEO of General Electric Co., said, "Good business leaders create a vision, articulate the vision, passionately own the vision and relentlessly drive it to completion."

For strategic planning purposes, leadership can be defined as a leader and leadership team arriving at a truly shared, inspiring vision and strategic plan that they are passionate about, can articulate to all stakeholders, and are willing to pursue undeterred by problems or setbacks.

The Leader Must Lead!

Whether they do it consciously or not, a leader establishes the vision for the organization, and the ethos and character of it. Thus, the more visionary and strategic the leader is, the better. This chapter describes the importance of leadership in general and especially its role in the process of developing a strategic plan. Many people confuse leadership with management and delegate the strategic planning process to a group of middle managers and analysts. Yet, if we believe the statement above about the leader and leadership team arriving at a truly shared and inspiring vision and strategic plan, then the leader must take the lead. That's the only way for the plan to reflect their vision and for them be completely committed to it.

Key Characteristics of Good Leaders

Since this is a book on strategic planning and we are passionate about passion, we will say, unequivocally that good leaders must have an excellent intellectual understanding of their organization and its business, and they must also have good hearts. They must appreciate and understand their people as human beings.

Later in the book (in Appendix 1), we discuss people's values. Leaders can have very different values and characteristics, just as their employees do, and those values will provide the backdrop to everything they do and say. However, we have identified some characteristics that appear to be common among the leaders with whom we have worked.

- They know themselves—their strengths, weaknesses, predilections, and "hot buttons."
- They have a strong character and unwavering integrity.
- They have a true sense of honor.
- They are courageous and always strive to do the right thing.
- They always lead by example.
- They show respect for everyone.
- They treat everyone as human beings.
- They see and understand the big picture; they can conceptualize.
- They think strategically and systemically.
- They deal with complexity, ambiguity, and uncertainty.

- They trust and use their intuition.

- They understand cultures as well as technology.

- They think in terms of effects and outcomes.

- They synthesize.

- They are trustworthy.

- They build trust, and inspire trust in others.

- They are willing to take the initiative and innovate.

- They are self-confident and self-sufficient.

- They are willing to learn.

- They are willing to empower people.

- They are able to tell stories and put things in context.

Expanding on the first of these characteristics, in *The Art of War*, says, "If you know the enemy and know yourself, you need not fear the result of a hundred battles." In the armed forces today, this is generally interpreted as meaning that a commanding officer should know what weapons the enemy has, where the enemy is located, and what he's likely to do. In today's boardroom, this generally means to know your competitor (enemy) and your customer. In neither case, is much attention given to "know yourself," yet this is critical for success.

Knowing yourself is an important part of personal, psychological growth, and it is beneficial for you, as a leader, to be aware of your propensities so that you can tell your colleagues and subordinates your preferences, and to ensure you have colleagues who can complement your capabilities. To aid in the process, it helps to ask yourself a few key questions (and perhaps even ask colleagues to help):

- Am I an optimist or a pessimist?

    When faced with a decision, do I generally think of the positive aspects of taking it, or do I generally think of the worst case scenario? How does this propensity affect my attitude towards risk?

- Am I an observer, reader, or listener?

  If I am gathering information in order to make some decision, do I prefer to bring people together to discuss the pros and cons, while I watch and listen to them? Do I like to read the facts and figures and mull over them in my own time? Do I prefer to close my eyes, sit back in my chair and listen to someone telling me the information. What is the most effective approach for me?

- Am I predominantly a thinker, doer, or feeler?

  Do I understand things or learn things by thinking about them and analyzing them? By rolling up my sleeves and learning by doing? Or by using my intuition/gut feelings? What does this do for my colleagues/subordinates?

- Am I extravert or introvert?

  Do I prefer to be around people, gaining ideas and energy from them, or do I prefer to be quiet and on my own? What is the most effective for my work?

- Am I focused on past, present, or future?

  Do I spend my time thinking about the way my organization has operated in the past – what made it successful, and how can we replicate those successes? Do I focus on the present and what is going well – doing more of what is making it successful and minimizing failures? Or do I focus on the vision and all the possibilities that we can work towards? What would be best for the organization?

- Is my time horizon short- or long-term?

  Is my focus on short-term results (monthly sales, for instance) or longer-term ones (the growth of the organization over the next 5 or even 25 years?)

- Am I concerned about the big picture, or details?

  Do I focus on developing the vision and strategies, or am I more concerned about the details of day-to-day operation? How might I compensate and make sure I can do both?

- Am I concerned about punctuality?

  If I am, then I expect the rest of the organization to be that way. If I am not, then I cannot expect the rest to be punctual.

- Am I concerned about meeting deadlines?

  If I am, then I expect the rest of the organization to be that way. If I am not, then I cannot expect the rest to meet deadlines.

- Am I a good communicator?
  Leaders need to be!

- Am I passionate or cool?

  Can I inspire people with my passion, or do I subdue them by being cool? How might I do more to inspire?

It is also very useful to write your own "leadership philosophy," which can be given to all your subordinates, or posted on your organization's website or blog. It should be no more than two pages long. In it, you describe your personal vision as the leader of the organization. You discuss your values and why they are important to you, and you describe the examples you intend to set. For instance, you might say, "I intend to set examples for you by practicing what I am asking of you—in terms of values, actions, and words. I intend to get the best out of you, preferably by encouragement and inspiration rather than punishment. I like to have fun and laughter in my organization." Discuss how you intend to operate—via a leader's intent, or tighter control—and stick to it! Operating by a leader's (or commander's) intent is where the leader tells people what is to be achieved, why it's to be achieved, but not HOW to do it. Some leaders want to micromanage with details of how, and this can kill creativity and improvisation. Tell people what you expect of them so they don't do things that irk you. For example, you might say you want punctuality, you want them to meet deadlines, and you want to know ahead of time if they are going to be late.

The Nature of Leadership

Leadership is different from management. The old adage says that leaders lead people, and managers manage things. Together, leadership and management develop shared intent to achieve coordinated action.

Leadership is as much an art as a science. It is the creative expression of the human will necessary to accomplish an organization's mission. Management is the control and administration of the structures and processes devised by the leadership to enable the organization to function effectively and to manage risk[1].

With that in mind, let's consider the function and necessary characteristics of leadership. Leadership in the business and even governmental world is slightly different from leadership in the Armed Forces. While the CEOs of private sector organizations are responsible to their boards and shareholders to grow their businesses and protect their share prices, commanding generals and admirals (and all those under their commands) are responsible to support and defend the U.S. Constitution against all enemies, foreign and domestic, and to bear true faith and allegiance to the same. This obligates such officers to a more personally disinterested, yet critical sense of duty. Good leaders in the private sector and other government agencies sometimes have this sense of duty to their shareholders, and other stakeholders, but it has not been seen as a primary consideration by many businesses, as we have seen in the tales of excess and greed on Wall Street over the last decade or so. However, we believe there is a lot that business can learn from the military approach to leadership. And while General George

---

1   Adapted from Pigeau and McCann, "Re-conceptualizing Command and Control," *Canadian Military Journal, Vol. 3, No. 1, Spring, 2002.*

Patton was in a category of "one-off" leaders all on his own, he still provides a great example of leadership—what it meant to him, how he carried it out, and why his troops were so loyal.

General George S. Patton was one of the finest generals and leaders[2]. He was regarded by politicians and some of his peers as a prima donna—and he was proud to be one—yet he was beloved by his troops. He understood the need to win. He understood and inculcated loyalty up and, more importantly, *down* the chain of command. He understood leaders must lead from the front—never asking others to do anything he wouldn't do himself. He gave sincere and generous praise to his troops in public, realizing that pride would motivate them and inspire an attitude of success. And he reprimanded in private. He believed the role of a commander was not to manage, but to command, to lead by example, never to show fear or doubt, and never to accept defeat. He had many, if not most, of the characteristics of good leadership that we list in the previous section.

He was a great believer in planning and contingency planning, yet he realized they could never be implemented perfectly. Indeed he said, "A good plan violently executed now is better than a perfect plan executed next week." A familiar corollary is that "a plan never survives contact with the enemy." Regardless, it's the process of planning that is most important—thinking strategically about the context and one's responses to it and actions in it. Risks are inherent in warfare—even more than in business—and Patton was a believer in taking calculated risks, yet not being rash.

He believed in education and training for himself and his troops, saying, "To lead is to teach." And he trained relentlessly, partly to ensure the entire command was ready for battle, and partly to create a strong team that could work together under any condition. He expected the world around him to change, and he wanted everyone to be prepared for it. He had a saying: "Keep moving, and the enemy cannot hurt you. You dig a foxhole, and you dig your grave." Many leaders claim they

---

2   This is a general overview from Alan Axelrod, *Patton on Leadership,* Prentice Hall, 1999.

are willing to change, yet, in reality, only in specific directions; they are not open to *any* kind of change. Yet we are living in times that demand flexibility and openness to change.

We have had experience in both the military and civilian worlds, and have brought the best of our experience in the military environment to bear on our civilian, commercial clients. For example, we teach that the more leaders can put the success of the organization above their personal success, the more likely both are to succeed, and the more loyalty they express *down* the chain of command, the greater the performance of their people and the greater loyalty that will be expressed upwards.

A leader's job is to guide the organization to success. This cannot be accomplished alone or without the cooperation of management, employees, and other stakeholders. *Thus a leader must be responsible for being the key visionary strategist, for developing the vision and mission, and for guiding the rest of the organization toward success.* That's not to say that the vision should not be developed in conjunction with others. Indeed, our approach is based on the top leadership team, together with some young mavericks, developing the vision. Mavericks are those young people in your organization who are constantly bubbling with ideas, which all too often never reach the ears of the leadership. As we have stated previously, sometimes leaders delegate the strategic planning process to a group of middle managers and analysts. That is a mistake and a way to lose control of their leadership responsibility. Leaders need to participate personally in the preparation of a strategic plan for it to reflect their vision and for them be completely committed to it. Key stakeholders may also be included in the planning process, if desired. Generally we do not recommend including middle managers unless they are part of a strategic planning group, as they do not have the experience and insights of the leadership or the disruptive, innovative ideas of mavericks. If the organization has a strategic planning group, then we recommend that it participates in the planning process to be able to help with subsequent implementation, but it should not take the lead.

Visionary Strategist

Good leaders are almost always visionary strategists. Indeed, the word "strategist" is derived from στρατηγός (strategos), the Greek word for leadership or generalship. It generally referred to the branch of military science dealing with military command and the planning and conduct of a war. In other words, it is a concept that encompasses large dimensions in space, time, resources, and desires. In transferring the concept to the civilian arena, it incorporates the ideas of large systems, frequently systems of systems that must operate together for the achievement of the vision and mission of the organization or concept. The reason we include the word "concept" in the last sentence is because strategic planning is necessary for concepts, as well as for organizations. Putting a man on the moon within 10 years was a visionary concept that had to be developed into a strategy that cut across many organizations, including the then relatively new National Aeronautics and Space Administration (NASA).

Indeed, visionary strategic planning can also be applied to marketing planning, new business development, and R&D planning. We've worked on many projects in these areas using the same processes that we use for organizational strategies.

We use the adjective "visionary" because we want to distinguish between large, organizational, or concept strategies, and those that are for smaller, short-term purposes, such as a brand strategy or communications strategy, or a strategy that is designed to overcome problems. That doesn't mean small organizations do not have visionary strategies. The owner of a family restaurant may have a vision for the future that includes a national or even global presence, which will benefit his family for generations to come. But that is very different from a restaurant opened to provide day-to-day income for a family and whose owner is content with that. Our VBP process can be used by any size and type of organization; it is highly scalable.

Leadership Styles

There has been a great deal written about leadership styles, which is why we are including a short description here. There are as many leadership styles as there are people. Most are based on the leader's values and education, and they form a "dominant" style. However, they are not fixed; they can and should change as circumstances and context require. Thus, leaders need to be aware of both their own propensities and what is required in the moment. In 1939, Kurt Lewin conducted a seminal study on leadership styles and identified three styles. Daniel Goleman (of emotional intelligence fame) has identified others, including Visionary, Coaching, Affiliative, and Pacesetting[3]. Transformational leadership was identified by James MacGregor Burns in 1978, and Servant Leadership was developed by Robert Greenleaf in 1970.

All these leadership styles have their pros and cons. There is no single correct approach for all circumstances. Rather, the good leader picks from among them as appropriate. In our experience, the most effective styles for getting things done are:

> *Visionary*, in which the leader encourages the leadership and management to develop and work toward a shared vision. To us, this is the most effective, and it can be used by mature organizations, as well as new ones to very good effect, to move them in new directions.

> *Democratic*, which draws on people's knowledge and skills, and creates a group commitment to the resulting vision and plan.

> *Authoritarian* (which is commonplace in military organizations), in which a single individual has the responsibility and accountability for his decisions.

---

3   Daniel Goleman and Richard Boyatzis *Primal Leadership: Unleashing the Power of Emotional Intelligence*, Tenth Anniversary Edition, Abridged, August 6, 2013.

Our workshop process relies heavily on the first two of these styles. In the example of General Patton, given earlier, it is clear that he had a combination of Visionary and Authoritarian styles.

Our conclusion is that good, effective leadership is critical for the development and implementation of a vision and strategic plan. Good leaders have certain characteristics and leadership styles, and current leaders and aspiring ones can better themselves by understanding what those are and why they are important.

Key Points from this Chapter

- Good leadership is critical for the success of any organization.

- A good leader knows their strengths, weaknesses, and predispositions.

- A good leader treats everyone with respect.

- There are different leadership styles that are appropriate for different circumstances and contexts.

- A good leader should be a visionary strategist—able to visualize the organization over space and time.

- It is useful for leaders to develop a two-page Leadership Philosophy that is posted on the organization's website or personal blog, to ensure that everyone in the organization understands what to expect.

PART II:
Preparation For The Workshop

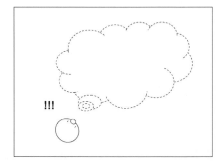

CHAPTER 4

Understanding the Organization Context and Environment

The Importance of Knowing Where We Are

Unless we know where we're at, we cannot establish a route for getting to where we want to be. It's like saying "I want to go to Denver." But if we're in Washington, DC, our route and direction is very different than if we're in San Diego. In this chapter, we discuss the kind of data collection and analysis that needs to be undertaken by organizations on a continuous basis, to establish where they are in the world, in the marketplace, and with respect to their competition and more, as well as for providing input into the Vision-Based Planning (VBP) process. Ideally, the organization will have conducted the kinds of analyses described below. In some cases, organizations do not know what they need, so they collect too little or too much. However, before we begin a VBP project, we want to make sure that specific information we know will be required is covered somewhere. So we conduct interviews with the leadership, key stakeholders, and we also obtain information from various external sources. This information needs to be realistic and honest, not a glossed-over account, or a wish list.

Initial Interviews

Prior to undertaking a VBP project with a client, we conduct extensive interviews with the leadership, key stakeholders, and some younger members of the organization. These younger people are likely to be the future of the organization, and they have a stake in its success. They are also more technologically savvy and less bound by tradition. Again, we always encourage the leadership to include some of their young mavericks as participants in their workshops.

During the interviews, we ask people how they see the organization. What business are you really in? Could you perceive it from some other perspective? What do you think are its strengths and weaknesses? What new areas of business could you see the organization moving toward? What and who do you see as major threats? What would you like to see done differently? Since we conduct the interviews in confidence, we encourage the interviewees to be honest and open in their remarks. However, we ask that any criticism be directed at a person's actions or words, not at the person themselves.

We also look at any analyses we can obtain from open sources, from other consultants who may have worked with, or produced reports on, that particular company or industry. We also conduct "serendipitous intelligence"—searching the internet and following our noses (aka intuition).

Although we perform this research prior to starting the VBP process, organizations should be analyzing their own operating environment and strategic context on a continuous basis. Some large organizations have a department that does this, others subscribe to various analytical services provided by outside data collection and analysis companies. In our experience, while some organizations do this very well, others have a "hit and miss" approach that can be an expensive proposition. We have seen organizations that subscribe to many data and analysis services, and commission "futures" and foresight projects, without any good way of collating and interpreting the information. The rest of this chapter as well as the following chapter provide guidance for what needs to be collected and analyzed, and how to do it effectively.

Analyzing the Strategic Context

This is a critical part of the planning process, and it needs to be done by the organization prior to the workshops, although we will conduct a brief analysis of our own as mentioned above. This is a perfect task for a staff group or strategic planning department. This part of the analysis is often known as STEP or STEEP because of the subjects it covers: social, technological, economic—and more recently environmental—and political data. All organizations should research every area, although the detailed subjects will be those that are specifically relevant to them. What we want them to do is to develop a comprehensive picture of their operating environment—all the things that might affect their organization and its business, and that might be affected by the organization. For instance, establishing a shopping mall requires an analysis of the following:

- Area population: their demographics, values, attitudes, lifestyles, disposable income.

- Geographic and geological considerations.

- Infrastructure considerations for the mall, including transportation, water, sewage, and power.

- State and local government policies, tax rates, and incentives.

The act of building the mall will have impact on the local area in terms of increase in land use, transportation, water and power use, the local physical environment, and more.

In preparation for the VBP, we recommend researching the following kinds of subjects:

- **Socio-cultural situation:** *What is happening that might impact the organization's operations/business?*
  - Changing values and attitudes of the population.
  - Changing demographics.
  - Changing attitudes toward the military, business, health and fitness, etc.
  - Increasing use of social media.

- New forms of influence.
- **Economic situation:** *What is happening that might impact the organization's business?*

  - Cuts in spending (defense, transportation, etc.)
  - More taxation on business.
  - Tax advantages for research and development (R&D).
  - Workforce education.
  - Changes in malpractice rules or legislation.
- **Political situation:** *What is happening that might impact the organization's business?*

  - Attitudes toward the military/defense.
  - Attitudes toward big business.
  - Changing political alliances.
  - Changes in legislation.
  - Wars and conflicts.
  - Changes in government-provided insurance.
  - Changes in international trade legislation.
  - Changes in government processes for acquisition approval.
- **Technology areas related to the business:**

  - New platforms and weapon systems.
  - Technologies for network-enabled capabilities.
  - The Internet of Things.
  - New technologies for Command, Control, Communications, Computers, and Intelligence, Surveillance, and Reconnaissance (C4ISR).
  - New developments in energy.
  - New personal health monitoring systems.
  - Many "early warning" systems and devices for areas such as counterfeiting, technological failure, and building security.
  - New logistics delivery systems.
  - Cyber-security.
- **The changing nature of future challenges:**

  - Increasing complexity.
  - Increasing globalization.

- Need for speed.
- Shortages of raw materials, energy.
- Shortages of food and water.
- Global pandemics.
- And many, many more.

SWOT Analysis

Conducting a SWOT (strengths, weaknesses, opportunities and threats) analysis can be useful, although we do not recommend spending a lot of time on it. This analysis tends to focus on micro-level issues, and for strategy we are more concerned with macro-level issues. Generally the leadership and management know what valid future SWOT concerns or issues (internal and external) they have. If they do have concerns, then a useful question to ask is: Are these underlying "root" concerns, or are they only symptoms of something deeper—and if so, what? The Socratic method of questioning can be useful to get at the deeper problem. Socratic questioning is a systematic, disciplined, and deep form of questioning of those who are knowledgeable about the subject, and it usually focuses on fundamental concepts, principles, theories, issues, or problems. However, if it seems difficult to think in these terms, here are some topics to get you started.

Strengths

Analysis of strengths can be done by examining your own organization, and asking yourself what you and the leadership think it is particularly good at.

- Generally we do not suggest a formal analysis process, but rather a discussion among the leadership.
- You can also analyze your strengths against your competitors'. This can be done by discussion, or by using the results of analyses and commentary from Wall Street or other analysts.

Weaknesses

These concerns are generally internal (or very closely related):

- Inability to attract young, qualified people.
- Lack of understanding of the global political situation.
- Lack of R&D capability.
- Reliance on a single supplier.
- Poor internal communications.
- Inability to communicate effectively with the government.
- Inability to communicate effectively with potential clients.

Opportunities

Opportunities can be found in many areas, but sometimes you may need to reframe your business concept to see new opportunities (we will discuss this later, in the context of the workshop):

- New alliances, including geographical, horizontal, or vertical extensions of your business.
- New technology developments.
- New, broader marketing or business opportunities.
- New product development.
- New ways of adding value.
- Potential relationships, such as other industries, services, allies, NGOs, universities.

Threats

Like opportunities, there are threats from many areas:

- From countries that are directly competitive.
- From new technologies that are similar to yours but cheaper (and include counterfeits, here).

- From organizations that attract better people.

- From organizations that are more cost effective.

- From organizations that are better at strategic communications.

- From potential competitive acquisitions or mergers.

- From potential competitive alliances and partnerships with other businesses, universities, etc.

Using This Information in Preparation for the VBP Workshop

We take all the information, or as much as we can, from our interviews and the SWOT analysis to design our workshops. Next, we enter our analysis, preparation, and detailed workshop design phase, which usually consumes 250 to 300 hours. We spend some considerable time thinking about the organization from different perspectives. We research the organization's field of business and think about opportunities and threats that are really "way out," including things that might not only surprise the organization, but its competitors too. From these we prepare sets of questions we want the organization's leadership and extended team of participants to answer during the course of the workshops. While we sometimes ask questions directly, we often find that indirect questioning provides more insight. (If this… then what…? Or what would you expect if…? Or if this were a movie, how would you expect the story to develop?)

We also want participants to make assessments of various elements in the organization, its STEEP or STEP categories, for instance. To do this, we prepare huge templates of different kinds, based on our understanding of the organization, on which the participants will draw mind maps, rate ideas, and assess capabilities. Most of the templates are visual and very "hands-on." We will describe them in greater detail in Chapter 9, which focuses on tools and techniques. They can serve as very useful visual descriptions, and having the participants work on them together, jostling elbows and laughing with each other, also helps to break down barriers and open up the discussion.

At the end of this session, as we frequently do, we have a "What's Missing?" question period, and while we do not always gain huge insights from it, there have been occasions when someone has identified a new issue that has been critically important.

Key Points from this Chapter

■ Your organization needs to understand where it's at before you can plan a route and strategy to get there.

■ To develop a comprehensive understanding of your organization and its operating environment, we recommend two major areas of analysis:

- STEEP: Examine Social, Technological, Economic, Environmental, and Political issues.
- SWOT: Look at your organization's major Strengths, Weaknesses, Opportunities and Threats.

■ Before the VBP workshop, you should conduct interviews with your leadership, some key stakeholders and mavericks.

■ Use information from the interviews to prepare questions and templates for use in the workshops.

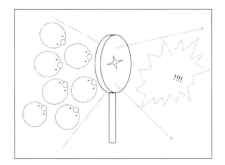

CHAPTER 5

Turning External Information into Actionable Intelligence

Good Intelligence is a Critical Requirement

As we mentioned at the beginning of the previous chapter, many organizations spend a great deal of money, time, and effort in collecting and/or purchasing data, and often bring in experts to provide further information. All this information can be very useful if it is used effectively, but in our experience much of it is wasted. This chapter provides insight into how your organization can make more effective use of all the data that is available to you.

Clearly, for effective strategic planning, the more we know about the future, the better. We need to be prepared. But when does preparation become overwhelming, or paralysis by analysis? This chapter starts with descriptions of the problems and pitfalls that can emerge from a seemingly beneficial data collection and analysis activity. It concludes with methods to prevent those pitfalls and ensure that the benefits of this activity can be found and implemented. *The problems generally stem from an assumption that information itself is intelligence. The solutions emerge from turning that information into actionable intelligence.*

Information from External Sources – Benefits and Problems

Many leaders believe that their leadership and management teams do not know enough about their strategic environment to enable them to make effective long-term decisions. This is particularly true of very large, complex, international and multinational organizations. Because of this, organizations will often subscribe to external environmental scanning services and commission global trend reports, or will put together an in-house foresight team to cull trends and develop these reports Or, prior to conducting a strategic planning process, they will invite subject matter experts to speak at their planning event. Sometimes they do all of these at considerable cost.

All these approaches can be useful, but they can also have their drawbacks, so they need to be handled with care. We have been involved in all these activities as report and event producers, speakers, and users, so we understand how to get the best out of all of them.

There are four key areas that should be considered when selecting external sources:

1. Who are the experts you will choose for your analysis and/or as speakers, and how might their perceptions be biased?

2. What the experts or foresight groups are going to say/report— do you select the subjects, or do they?

3. How are they going to report their findings—reports, presentations, spreadsheets, graphic representations, models?

4. Are those insights likely to be useful for your organization?

Speakers

Let's start with speakers, as they are the most frequently used external experts. When you select a speaker, make sure they are an expert in an area that is relevant to your organization and the information to be given in the presentation is in a form you can use.

Say your organization is thinking about developing some new products and expanding its markets into India and China. You have heard that Dr. X is a world-renowned expert on India, and Professor Y has helped many similar organizations develop markets in China. You decide that, when your organization holds its strategic planning meeting, you will invite Dr. X to give a 40-minute keynote presentation first thing in the morning, followed by a 20-minute discussion. Then you will invite Professor Y to do the same thing over lunch. In the time between Dr. X's speech and Professor Y, there will be an overview of the past year's performance, and the VPs for business development and marketing will give their perspectives on the new products and the potential for the new market areas. Following lunch with Professor Y, the executives will reconvene—perhaps breaking into small groups—with each group focused on some aspect of the new products or new market development.

Meeting day arrives, and Dr. X gives his morning presentation. He really knows his stuff, and it is a fascinating lecture. However, it is about the socio-political relationships between various regions in India, and although he does his best to bring in some elements of trade and international business, he doesn't say much that is relevant to the company's business. And the 20-minute Q&A period does not provide the executives enough time to get into some of the details that they would like to hear. After Dr. X's presentation, they go back to their meeting agenda and get on with their business.

At lunchtime, Professor Y is more attuned to business interests in China, but the lunchtime speech, interrupted by food, is too short, and the 20-minute Q&A is also too short to get into details that are relevant.

Worse, still, what few people realize is that presentations put people into a passive, receptive mode—some psychologists would call it a trance. This is particularly true when combined with food. So when people return to what is supposed to be the active, working part of the meeting, they are in a frame of mind that is the opposite of what is wanted: active, creative, and interactive.

Perhaps even more important, there is no place on the agenda to discuss how what they have heard from Dr. X and Professor Y applies to their business and what the implications might be. Perhaps some people may have gleaned an idea or two from the presentations, but on the whole, two hours of a large number of executives' time have effectively been wasted, and the fees paid to the two experts have been significant.

In summary, including "expert speakers" in workshops is generally counterproductive, and we discourage the practice. More will be said about this later, in the "solutions" section of this chapter.

Environmental Scanning and Foresight

These two areas are closely related, so we will discuss them together. Sometimes they are conducted internally if the organization is large enough to be able to afford a team devoted to these areas. If not, there are consultancies that specialize in these areas, frequently through subscription services. In these cases, the consultancies will conduct some general environmental scanning and foresight studies, and then develop a customized report for each of their clients.

In general, environmental scanning is conducted by analysts who scour the operating environment (STEEP as in the previous chapter) for information about the future—trends, events, changes, and so on. Before they start, the analysts need some frame of reference. How should they categorize the scanning? Are they going to look for information by regions of the world? Or by broad disciplines (social, technological, economic, political, other)? Or by categories that are particularly meaningful to their clients' nation or organization? Frequently horizon scanning is conducted prior to an organization developing its strategic plan. Some of that can be very useful in thinking about the future environment in which the organization will be operating. However, if it is conducted at this stage – prior to the planning – then the directions given to the scanners will be based on the historical trends and current circumstances of the organization. We prefer to conduct the planning in the creative and imaginative way, using the methods described in Chapter 9, especially using reframing techniques for the organization, and *then* conduct the scanning based on this new perspective of the organization. So, for instance, if we are thinking about a project to look at The HOUSE of the Future, then we would want to scan for developments in urban planning, building materials, construction techniques, infrastructure, power/energy, waste disposal, appliances, consumer electronics, furniture, furnishings...and so on. If we were to reframe it into the HOME of the Future, then it would include those areas *and* a whole lot more, such as trends in working from home—the need for office space that is appropriately designed to accommodate office equipment, office and communications technology, improved sound insulation, ... If trends of working from home, more homes in rural areas to be closer to nature or to get away from urban sprawl, and home schooling all converge, then the home will need facilities for home schooling, for more entertainment, more need for fitness equipment, and perhaps for monitoring family-members' health situations. (The Internet of Things would be very useful here!) So you could ask yourself what additional things should the horizon scanners be looking for?

Then the organization and analysts need a means for pulling all this information into a coherent report—often through the use of scenarios. Scenarios, as we use them, are postulated sequences of events put together into stories about the future of an organization. They are organization-specific, so we cannot provide an example. However, there are many publications of global scenarios that outline stories of the way the world may develop. For example, in 2013, the U.S. Intelligence Community (IC) produced a *Global Trends 2030* report that described several global scenarios.

This is where the scanning turns into foresight. These scenarios may have quantitative and qualitative elements to them, and they may be developed through the use of discussion and narratives by expert analysts, or through complex computer models. But one of the key elements to remember in this activity is "the map is not the territory," a phrase coined by Alfred Korzybski to illustrate the differences between belief and reality. Another key element is that the people collecting the information and conducting the analyses tend to be from a single culture or related cultures, and therefore they perceive the information and its relevance from a particular perspective. What may be interpreted one way from the perspective of an analyst may be seen quite differently by a business executive or a commander on the ground. And so, even though analysts may sometimes be asked to provide implications of their findings, they may not be appropriate because they do not have the relevant background and frequently do not see the big picture.

To do environmental scanning properly and thoroughly is time-consuming and very expensive. For example, in 2013, the IC produced the *Global Trends 2030* report mentioned above. It was an interesting and very well-presented glossy document that had been prepared by a team within the IC working with a well-known consultancy. It was rolled out with some fanfare and presentations. I am sure that the people who conducted the analyses had looked at their respective areas in great depth and had a thorough understanding of their sections of the report. I am also sure that there were still questions the analysts would have liked to have worked on further and questions they had to leave unanswered because of time constraints. Another difficulty is that world events do not stand still and, because such studies take time, some of the conclusions may be outdated before the study is finished.

Finally, all the analyses have to be condensed into a readable document. The final report—and I am sure this is true of all reports prepared this way—was weak. It didn't say anything "new," or revolutionary. It didn't even raise questions that strayed from conventional wisdom. And where it gave the implications of its findings they, too, were minimal.

So what are you to do with such a report? The obvious solution is for you and your leadership team to read it, even though it may not contain all the details. Some people do read the whole report, but the majority only read the executive summary, which is even less detailed and more lackluster. This is a waste of time, money, effort, and valuable expertise.

Solutions for Getting Information from External Sources

Speaker Solutions

If you believe your leadership and management team needs an external speaker who will provide information that the rest of the organization needs to hear, or a speaker who will provide a different perspective than that held by people in the organization, then you need to identify such a speaker very carefully. As in the example given above, it shouldn't be someone who is an expert on, say India or China, it needs to be an expert who can provide answers to the particular problems and questions that the organization needs to address for doing business with each of those countries. These may be questions related to available resources— human as well as material; to government policies regarding business ownership and taxation; problems with counterfeiting, piracy, terrorism; or a myriad more.

Once a speaker is identified, it not good enough to ask that expert to provide a 45-minute presentation. You need to prepare a proper brief for the speaker, explaining your problems and requirements. Then you need to discuss with the speaker exactly what you want to get out of both the presentation and the Q&A. And, ideally, you want the speaker to provide a short paper that describes the key points of the presentation. The leadership and managers who will be attending the presentation need to be briefed. They have business interests in India and China, for instance. What specifically do they need to know? You might ask them to write down questions, send them to you so you can provide them to the speaker, or bring them to the presentation, so if they have the opportunity to ask their question, it will be brief and concise.

Then—and this is the most important part—*you need to turn what the speaker has said into actionable intelligence.* Immediately after the speaker has left, you, your leadership, and managers should discuss the key points you have heard and identify the main implications for the business. Ideally, the group needs to set aside 60 to 90 minutes for this discussion. This may seem like a lot, but if an organization is going to benefit from the speaker's knowledge, it needs to take the time to digest it. Then, and only then, is it OK to move to the next step on the agenda.

One final point about speakers: We mentioned earlier that, when listening to speakers, participants are in a passive, receptive mode. When they are working on strategic planning, they need to be active, creative, and engaged. When we bring in speakers to our workshops, be they external or internal speakers, *we hold all the presentations the day before the workshop begins* so the participants can be actively focused and engaged for everything else.

Environmental Scanning and Foresight Solutions

When our clients have subscribed to an environmental scanning service, or have purchased a global trends report from an external source, or if they have had their own department provide such a report, prior to the planning process, then we take a similar approach to the one we employ with speakers.

We insist that you and every member of the leadership and management team that is going to participate in one of our strategy or futures workshops reads the whole report—and thinks about it. We ask each participant to consider the implications of each major section of the report, the scenarios (if provided), and the report as a whole. Then, before we get into the main work of the workshop, we hold sessions to explore and discuss the implications of what they have read. If we think there are areas missing from the report we will add them, either by ourselves or through other experts. *In other words, we are helping the organization turn the report into actionable intelligence.* Only then do we continue with the rest of our workshop. This approach is the sensible thing to do. Why do organizations prepare or purchase such reports, if they are not going to take them seriously?

As mentioned above, we believe it can be useful for an organization to undertake or purchase an environmental scanning program or a trends report prior to conducting major strategic planning or futures activities, as they lay the groundwork for what follows. However, you do not need to do this very often, perhaps only every three or five years or so. Rather, our recommendation is that, once the strategic plan has been prepared and developed in a WarRoom, which is a way of making information and intelligence actionable (as discussed in Chapter 9), then an internal group (planning or foresight) should scan on a regular basis for emerging trends, events, and circumstances that could counter the assumptions made in the strategic planning process. When they find some issue, event, trend, or circumstance of concern, then they should prepare all necessary documentation, and provide it to you and the leadership team, with a detailed explanation of the implications, including where and how its impact can be seen in the WarRoom.

In other words, rather than a foresight group preparing a detailed report of miscellaneous analyses at frequent intervals, a much better use of its time and efforts is to be more focused on what you and your organization need to know to ensure that you can achieve your vision and strategies. And should it appear that certain trends are going to push it off-course, then focus on analyses of what you might do to counter or adjust to the trends, or calculate a new direction. *Focus* and *implications* should be the hallmarks of any futures and foresight activities.

Key Points from this Chapter

■ Experts as speakers can be useful, but make sure you invite those who actually have something to contribute to *your* organization.

- Describe to them what you are looking for—what subjects need to be covered.
- Ask them to prepare a short paper, or at least key points of what they will be saying.
- Ask your leaders and managers to prepare questions, and bring them in writing to the presentation.

■ Scanning and foresight can be useful, but make sure that the analysts or service providers are scanning and analyzing useful, relevant material. You don't want to end up with a data dump.

■ Allow adequate time to discuss and turn all the information from the speakers and reports into actionable intelligence.

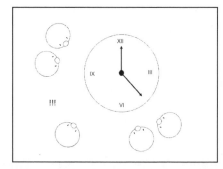

CHAPTER 6

Timing Aspects of Workshop Design

How Long Should a Workshop Take?

There is a lot to accomplish in a strategic and vision planning workshop, and many people do not allow enough time to accomplish their goals. This chapter will provide some guidelines for planning and executing an effective workshop.

Plenary Sessions/Whole Group Sessions

The main purpose of plenary sessions is to inform. In this type of session, the format is that of a conference or seminar with one speaker or a panel that is speaking to the whole audience. If there is time following the presentation, then the audience may ask questions or make comments. This is a standard approach for starting a workshop. Think of it like an orientation, when all the participants need to be informed about what is going to take place.

In plenary sessions, the intake—or "data rate"—is very slow, and everything takes place sequentially. We do not recommend plenary sessions for exploration of ideas.

Plenary sessions can also take place during or after a workshop in which the large group has been divided into two or more small groups in order to work in parallel. Working in small groups increases the data rate significantly, and it enables every participant to have a say, which increases commitment to the end result. In this type of format, each group has a few minutes to brief the results of their group discussions to the other groups, and a few minutes for questions. Then, if there is time at the end, there is a short, general discussion of all the groups' results from their working sessions.

Small Group Sessions

Small group sessions are usually convened to explore a range of ideas, concepts, issues, situations, implications, and so forth. The keyword is usually "exploration." They accomplish more results by working in parallel, they make best use of people's expertise and interests, and they ensure that everyone has the opportunity to make their ideas known. They also provide the individuals with more time to get their ideas across and, since people like to speak, they feel as though they have accomplished more—and therefore are more committed to the outcomes.

Small groups can range from 2 to 10 people; the ideal number is about seven. However, due to time constraints, we sometimes have to trade off smaller numbers for time, as we will explain later. In our workshops, we sometimes have many different sizes and numbers of groups—sometimes up to six or seven groups working in parallel—so we have to ensure we have enough time for them to work on the topic and to present their findings to each other. The paragraphs below provide some guidelines about how to structure times.

There is frequently a debate among ourselves as the consulting team, and/or with our clients about how to structure the small groups. Say we have six topics to address: Is it better for all the groups to work on all six topics at the same time, or for two groups to work on three different topics each, or for three groups to work on two topics each? In the case of *all* groups working on *all* the topics, we get a greater breadth of ideas covered on each topic, since each group will have a slightly different perspective; however, time constraints mean they can only cover them very shallowly. When each group works on different topics in the same time, the results lack the different perspectives mentioned above, but they have much greater depth. We will illustrate this with numbers later.

There are three considerations for small group sessions:

- How the topics cluster, if at all.
- The desired range of exploration (breadth and depth).
- How much time there is for the whole workshop.

One additional consideration is the time it takes a group to decide what it is going to do about the topic and how it will do it. This occurs even when the subject is described in detail, as in our worksheets (which we explain in detail in Chapter 9.) That time can range from 5 to 15 minutes. Many people forget this occurs. However it needs to be taken into account in the timing.

Following the small group sessions, there should be plenary sessions in which the groups present their top/key results to each other. Ideally, a Q&A should take place after each presentation, and time allotted for some kind of general discussion, or even a synthesis of the results.

Typically, a small group session will look like this:

5-10 minutes: Participants decide what to do and how to do it.

XX minutes: Discuss/explore topic (actual work time).

10 minutes: Prioritize ideas and prepare for briefing.

Now that you have the basics, let's look at the two approaches to small group sessions. For illustration purposes, we will assume two groups, six topics, and approximately seven hours of working time (given breaks and lunch). We have not included breaks other than lunch here.

Approach 1: Each Group Works on All 6 Topics

Each topic gets a total of 30 minutes of working time from each group, plus 15 minutes of briefing, Q&A, and discussion for each group. Table 6-1 illustrates this.

	GROUP A	GROUP B
0800-0845	Topic 1: actual work 30 min	Topic 1: actual work 30 min
0845-0915	PLENARY BRIEFINGS Each group 7 min brief & general	& Q/A ON TOPIC 1 5 min Q/A plus 6 mins discussion
0915-1000	Topic 2: actual work 30 min	Topic 2: actual work 30 min
1000-1030	PLENARY BRIEFINGS Each group 7 min brief & general	& Q/A ON TOPIC 2 5 min Q/A plus 6 mins discussion
1030-1115	Topic 3: actual work 30 min	Topic 3 —actual work 30 min
1115-1145	PLENARY BRIEFINGS Each group 7 min brief & general	& Q/A ON TOPIC 3 5 min Q/A plus 6 mins discussion
1145-1300	LUNCH	LUNCH
1300-1345	Topic 4: actual work 30 min	Topic 4 — actual work 30 min
1345-1415	PLENARY BRIEFINGS Each group 7 min brief & general	& Q/A ON TOPIC 4 5 min Q/A plus 6 mins discussion
1415-1500	Topic 5: actual work 30 min	Topic 5 — actual work 30 min
1500-1530	PLENARY BRIEFINGS Each group 7 min brief & general	& Q/A ON TOPIC 5 5 min Q/A plus 6 mins discussion
1530-1615	Topic 6: actual work 30 min	Topic 6 — actual work 30 min
1615-1645	PLENARY BRIEFINGS Each group 7 min brief & general	& Q/A ON TOPIC 6 5 min Q/A plus 6 mins discussion
1645-1700	WIND-UP	SESSION

Table 6-1: Each Group Works on All 6 Topics

STRATEGY WITH PASSION

Approach 2: Each Group Works on 3 Different Topics

Each topic gets 75 minutes working time, plus 30 minutes briefing, Q&A, and discussion for each group. Table 6.2 illustrates this.

	GROUP A	GROUP B
0800-0930	Topic 1: actual work 75 min	Topic 4: actual work 75 min
0930-1030	PLENARY BRIEFINGS Each group 10 min brief general	& Q/A ON TOPICS 1, 4 & 10min Q/A plus 20 mins discussion
1030-1200	Topic 2: actual work 75 min	Topic 5: actual work 75 min
1200-1330	LUNCH	LUNCH
1330-1430	PLENARY BRIEFINGS Each group 10 min brief general	& Q/A ON TOPICS 2, 5 & 10min Q/A plus 20 mins discussion
1430-1600	Topic 3: actual work 75 min	Topic 6: actual work 75 min
1600-1645	PLENARY BRIEFINGS Each group 10 min brief general	& Q/A ON TOPICS 3, 6 & 10min Q/A plus 20 mins discussion
1645-1700	WIND-UP	SESSION

Table 6-2: Each Group Works on 3 Different Topics

For every extra group added to either of these schedules, we have to subtract time from the group's working time, the briefings, Q&A, and discussion to keep to the 0800 start and 1700 finish times.

So for groups of up to 20 people, we usually recommend breaking into two small groups. If there are more than 20 people, we recommend dividing into three or four groups. But the trade-off is you lose time for the working/exploration and for the outbriefs/discussion, unless you extend the workshop beyond a single day.

Recommendations

One-day workshops are hardly worth the time and effort, especially if people are traveling long distances to get there. The tables above do not include any kind of plenary presentations to set the scene. If such presentations are included in the day, then obviously the time for working sessions is reduced. At the very least, we recommend short workshops to start with plenary presentations the afternoon or evening before, since, as we mention in Chapter 5, we want the participants to be actively engaged for the workshops, not in a passive mode. Then the day of the workshops consists mostly of small group working sessions with plenary discussions following them.

In addition, we find that the output from two- to three-day workshops is far greater than two- or three single-day workshops as there is more continuity and the participants do not have to spend time recalling what they have done previously. In other words, the participants build momentum that does not occur in single day sessions. And, as we mentioned in Chapter 5, speaking presentations should be kept separate from working sessions, and should preferably take place in late afternoon or evening sessions.

Key Points from this Chapter

- Timing is absolutely critical for the success of a workshop.
- Don't waste your time with one-day workshops.
- Calculate the time you want to have participants spend on topics *before* you decide on the length and structure of the workshops. You can always cut it back, but consider the ideal amount first.
- Decide on the number of plenary versus small group sessions, but remember to add in briefing/discussion time. And consider breadth versus depth.

PART III:
Vision-Based Planning Process

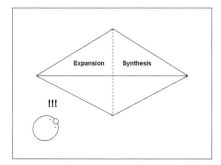

CHAPTER 7

Introduction to the 11 Step VBP Process

Vision-Based Planning is one of the Most Productive Activities an Organization can Undertake

Among the grumbles we hear about strategic planning are comments about the time it takes away from "productive work." Or the time it takes to produce a plan—apparently sometimes as much as a year. And the fact that, by the time the plan is completed, things will have changed.

This is nonsense! Our Vision-Based Planning (VBP) process takes leadership and top management all the way from vision and values to action and implementation in 11 easy steps over a period of no more than two three-day workshops. It is energizing, inspirational, and it can be a lot of fun. OK, so someone or some group has to prepare for the workshops and write up the findings afterward, but the whole effort can be accomplished in 8 to 12 weeks. The biggest problem usually is the scheduling of the workshops.

In fact, in separate projects for two different government organizations, two senior members told us in almost identical words: "I usually hate off-sites, but this is the best and most productive off-site I have ever attended."

VBP in a Nutshell

VBP is a unique approach to strategic planning, created and refined by us over the years, that allows a leadership team to create the strategy and plans for an organization or a concept around a vision that is truly shared and passionately embraced by the leadership of the organization.

It requires a combination of keen intellect and creativity, a willingness to see the organization (or concept) from different perspectives, and a willingness to change. There are two distinct parts to our VBP process: The first is expansionary and exploratory, and the second is synthesizing and converging, as indicated in Figure 7-1. This is a diagram we use to describe, briefly, the two parts of the process and the key elements that go into the expansionary phase, as well as the key outputs from the synthesis.

We have found that the 11 steps in our process can be accomplished best by the leader and the leadership team working together in workshop fashion. Typically, a VBP process for a complex organization takes two three-day workshops, as mentioned above—one for the Expansion and Exploration Phase, and one for the Synthesis Phase—each separated by no more than two weeks, with the top leadership participating in the whole of the event. As noted in Chapter 3, we recommend that a few mavericks also participate in the workshop and perhaps some key stakeholders in your organization. If the organization has a strategic planning group, those people should also participate.

We bring up the notion of mavericks again, because, due to their perspective on the organization—looking up from near or at the bottom of the hierarchy—they often bring up some of the best ideas for improvements, and participation in the workshop ensures that leadership hears them.

Stakeholders, as we use the term here, are generally people outside the organization, who have a stake in its future success and can contribute as a participant in the planning process. Consider inviting negative stakeholders as well as the cheerleaders. Negative stakeholders fall into two categories: those who criticize and complain about you and your organization, and those who stand to benefit from your failure to succeed. The former group can be useful to you because of their unique perspective; the latter are not. Be sure you know what sort of stakeholders they are before you extend an invitation.

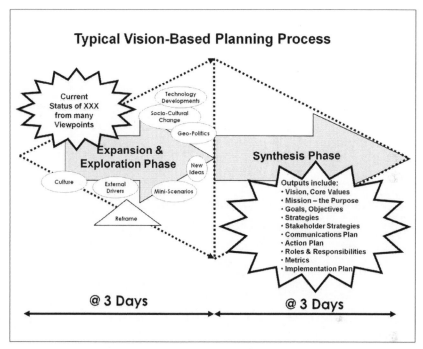

Figure 7-1: Our VBP Process

For VBP to be successful, we feel very strongly that the senior leadership *must* participate. As we remarked to one senior figure in one of the Armed Services, "If the senior leadership can't spend 2% of its time thinking about the future of this Service, who the hell else will?" Middle managers generally do not have the breadth of understanding or a sufficiently long-term perspective to be able to develop the vision and strategic plan, and sometimes because they have "been there, done that" they may try to obstruct change.

In our experience, too often, strategic plans are developed by a committee/strategic planning group that then has to "sell" its results to an organizational hierarchy that doesn't understand or own the assumptions that were made. Without personal ownership, the leadership often rejects the plans or pays only lip-service to them, and nothing gets done. These groups should *not* be responsible for generating the strategic plan; rather they should participate in the workshops and then be responsible for helping the rest of the organization implement the plan generated by the leadership.

We have found a workshop approach to be the fastest and most effective approach to developing, coordinating, and disseminating strategies for large complex organizations. For our purposes, a workshop is defined as an intensive, interactive session with the leadership, designed to achieve some practical and actionable result.

The workshop venue is best for the following reasons:

- You, your leadership team, and stakeholders can work together to produce shared results (reaching a genuine consensus) to which all of you will be committed. Since the results are yours, you are going to be enthusiastic about implementing them.

- Working in this way enables you and the project team to consider the views of large numbers of key people in parallel, which enables the team to produce its results quickly.

- Interactive work is one of the most effective ways to generate new and innovative ideas through cross-fertilization of experience and discipline.

- Each participant knows his/her voice has been heard; this minimizes discontent and maximizes buy-in.

- The issues raised by the different corporate or national cultures and the methods of the various members of the leadership or stakeholders are worked on together in the context of developing the shared vision and strategies.

- Participation in the workshops leads to improved communication, trust, and team-building among the participants.

As mentioned above, by sharing their different perspectives, you and the other participants develop a robust vision and strategies to which all of you are committed. In addition to the production of the vision and strategies, we design the workshop so all of you develop a systems' view of your organization and its operations. This enables you to see it as a whole so you can consider options for improving the management structure, organizational structure, and business performance.

In building this systems' view, all of you work on such topics as the organization's vision, its purpose or mission, its responsibilities, its values, the role of leadership, and the internal stakeholders. You also look at expectations, needs, values and visions of key individuals, and what all these may mean for the organizational structure, training and development. In situations involving key external stakeholders or part-nerships, we consider the cultures, and the requirements and concerns of each stakeholder or partner. Any problems facing the organization or partnership, or which are preoccupying the leadership are also solved or resolved in the workshop process. The participants spend consid-erable time addressing the issues of all external stakeholders and the means by which those stakeholders' needs can be satisfied. External stakeholders include such groups as customers, suppliers, and political organizations. You also develop measures and metrics, objectives and milestones to ensure that you can assess their effectiveness and perfor-mance in achieving the vision and outcomes.

The design of the workshop is key to producing the required results. We combine our knowledge of strategy and strategic plan-ning, together with our capabilities in facilitation and group dynamics, to produce workshops that are intensive, interactive, and productive. We use a combination of analytical and problem-solving techniques ("left-brained" techniques) together with psychological and creative ("right-brained") techniques. This combination of approaches enables all of you to see your organization from different perspectives and to "get-out-of-the-box."

Each workshop is outcome-focused. The design of each workshop is unique and based on extensive discussions and interviews with the client's leadership. Each day of the workshop is designed in 30- to 60-minute sessions or segments, each of which contributes directly and visibly to the desired output. Yet if we become aware of problems that did not surface earlier, we are flexible enough to be able to take the time to work on them. At the end of the workshop, all of you are asked to grade yourselves on such topics as level of understanding of the vision and strategic plan; level of understanding of what each of you and/or your organizations need to do to further the vision; and personal commitment to the vision and strategic plan.

We've had many clients say that our workshops have been the most productive they have ever attended; the results are produced extremely quickly, and yet they are enduring. For one military organization we supported, the vision and plan lasted for 14 years with only minor changes—a situation almost unheard of, when the leadership changes every two years.

In planning the workshop, we specify both plenary (full group) sessions and small group sessions designed so everyone will spend some time working with everyone else. This technique contributes very effectively to team building and improved communications. The nature and composition of the groups depends on the structure of the organization, your leadership group, stakeholders and partners, and the nature of the problems and issues facing it. There are no passengers in our workshops! Everyone participates, and everyone gets "air time."

One word of caution: Most people underestimate the time it takes to conduct a workshop session. We are frequently shocked by large organizations that tell us they want to hold a one-day workshop to discuss a subject of critical importance. It is ludicrous to imagine that 30 to 50 people can spend one day together and arrive at any useful results. We have discussed this topic in some detail in Chapter 6.

A workshop session requires time for the discussion by small groups, plus the time for presentations from each small group, and then a discussion of the presentations. The more small groups, the more time is needed for presentations and discussion. Chapter 6 provides guidance in the timing aspect of workshop design.

During the workshop, from shortly after the first session begins through to the end of the session, we prepare a draft WarRoom that we display around the room. This enables participants to see what they have produced and to follow the logic trail through the process as they go.

A Return to Consensus, not Compromise

One of the main benefits of the VBP approach is that it generates true consensus. We mentioned this difference between the two concepts in Chapter 2; however, it is worth revisiting here.

Consensus means to be in accord—in harmony—in opinion.

A *compromise* is a settlement of differences by arbitration or by consent reached by mutual concessions.

True consensus is powerful because it means that those who have arrived at a consensus will be willing to do what it takes to achieve the highest level of vision and mission that the group has defined. If you and your leadership are involved in developing the consensus, then you will be passionate about it—you will, as we say, "do it like you mean it."

In a compromise, the vision and mission are likely to be smaller in scope, since people have conceded some aspects of their desires. They are less likely to be willing to do what it takes because they are not wholeheartedly passionate about the result. This is one key element of the "head and heart" combination described in Chapter 1.

Our 11-Step VBP Process

Expansion Phase:

Step 1: Identify and understand the strategic context.

Step 2: Analyze issues, concerns, and problems of the organization today and into the future.

Step 3: Identify possible/potential desired directions for the organization using creative and imaginative techniques.

Participants then have a gap of two days to two weeks between sessions to enable them to mull over the ideas. We recommend the workshops take place Wednesday through Friday, with a gap over the weekend, and then resume Monday through Wednesday. That way, the momentum that has been gained is not lost.

Synthesis Phase:

Step 4: Develop the Vision and Values.

Step 5: Develop the Mission or Purpose.

Step 6: Develop Top-Level Strategic Goals.

Step 7: Develop Objectives to achieve goals.

Step 8: Develop Strategies to achieve each objective.

Step 9: Develop an Action Plan (measures, metrics, timeline, and assign roles and responsibilities).

Step 10: Develop an Implementation Plan (assign roles, responsibilities).

Step 11: Develop a Communications Plan.

In the remainder of Part 3, we will describe the elements of our workshop process for VBP in more detail.

Key Points from this Chapter

- Strategic planning should be fast, easy and fun—if it isn't, you're not doing it right!

- A workshop approach is the fastest and most effective approach to accomplish strategic planning.

- It requires your leadership and management team to work together.
  - This gives them opportunities to discuss the business in depth that they would normally never have.
  - It helps them become a cohesive team with a truly shared vision and values.
  - It is all based on consensus, never on compromise.

- This process has 11 easy steps that act as building blocks—if you go through the steps, you will have a complete strategic plan.

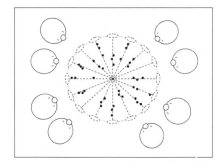

CHAPTER 8

Workshop, Phase 1: The Expansion Phase

Potential and Possibilities

The future is about potential and possibility, not regurgitation of the past. This is the most important and least understood, part of the VBP workshop process. Planning is not about making the future look like the past, it's about possibilities and potential, and that requires creativity and imagination. Our processes for doing this are covered in Steps 1-3 of our VBP process.

Step 1: Identify and understand the strategic context.

Step 2: Analyze issues, concerns, and problems of the organization today and into the future.

Step 3: Identify possible/potential desired directions for the organization using creative and imaginative techniques.

Although this phase is the most important part of the process, most people tend to omit it. While they generally perform some STEP or STEEP analyses as mentioned earlier, it is almost always conducted as an intellectual or analytical process. Our approach is imaginative and creative. We want people to get out of the box, to use their imaginations to visualize the future, to use all their senses and discover passion for the ideas and concepts. We also want them to experience the camaraderie and fun of working together.

Sometimes our clients who are engineers or military officers want to gloss over this step. They ask us: "When will we start work on the vision and plan?" or "When will we get to the *real* work?" Yet after they have gone through the process, they realize their minds did expand and they did develop new ideas. They saw things differently. And in some cases, even though it was not designed as part of the process, new ideas for technologies and systems emerged from the workshops. They also learned more about themselves and each other—both key elements of working together toward a shared vision.

We do not necessarily take these three steps sequentially, although we cover the content of all three in the course of this phase. That is why we have not listed each step in turn in this Chapter. Part of the process requires that we view and examine various aspects of the organization and its environment from different perspectives. For instance, we often cycle between semi-analytical and creative techniques. One of the critical parts is to ensure that you and your leadership team takes a comprehensive approach to evaluating the strategic environment. We often find that people want to focus on technology or the competition at the expense of understanding social and political aspects of the environment. Understanding people is crucial, whatever the nature of the organization. After all, people are responsible for developing and using technology, people fuel the economy by buying and selling what they choose, and people vote for politicians and their policies.

Imagination and the Future

One of the most important aspects of understanding people is to realize that they do not act solely on the basis of logic. In some cases, many more than most people realize, imagination and creativity take over.

No one can analyze the future. There are no data available—and thus we cannot use pure analytical techniques for this part of the process—which is why we have developed semi-analytical techniques ourselves or use those developed by others. We can extrapolate from the past, develop models and simulations, and develop scenarios about the future. But it is all speculation. We can give it the illusion of more accuracy by associating numbers with the speculations and analyzing the outcomes but, at the end of the day, it is all what we used to call SWAGs (sophisticated-wild-assed guesses).

This is not necessarily a bad thing. It can be bad, if people do not realize the limitations of the speculations, and act as if they were dealing with facts. But it can also be a hugely freeing and creative endeavor, if we realize that our imaginations are powerful. Every invention and innovation started as someone's wild idea or dream.

August Kekulé, the father of the theory of chemical structure, got his idea for the structure of benzene rings after daydreaming in front of a fire. In the flames, he saw an image of a snake seizing its own tail. As a teenager, Albert Einstein imagined chasing after a beam of light, and he believed that visualization played a significant role in his development of the theory of special relativity.

Steve Jobs made several interesting observations related to people and creativity. "Creativity is just connecting things," he said. "When you ask creative people how they did something, they feel a little guilty because they didn't really do it; they just saw something. It seemed obvious to them after a while. That's because they were able to connect experiences they've had and synthesize new things. It's not a faith in technology. It's faith in people." Generally, a group of people focused on the future can connect and expand on many more ideas than one person working alone – as described in our Home of the Future project, in Chapter 9.

Mature organizations, with mature technologies and processes, can benefit from all these ideas, just as much as high-tech start-ups. Mature organizations that can get a power boost from new and creative ideas—either internally or through new strategic alliances—can experience a real resurgence, as a number of MIT studies have shown.[4, 5]

---

4   Richard M. Locke and Rachel L. Wellhausen (Eds) *Production in the Innovation Economy*, MIT Press, January 2014.

5   Suzanne Berger, *Making in America: From Innovation to Market*, MIT Press, January 2014.

Intuition and The Art of Decision-Making

Most people (in the West, at least) think about decision-making as something of a science. We accumulate as much information as we can. We assemble it, analyze it, weigh the pros and cons, prioritize it, and eventually make our decisions. Then we pat ourselves on the back for having done the best we could to make the correct decision.

However, many recent studies, such as one conducted in a joint research study from the Kellogg School of Management and Nijmegen University, have indicated that a combination of analysis and intuition provides the best solutions to solving complex problems.[6] Over a decade ago, research psychologist Gary Klein wrote a seminal work on intuition—how to develop it, apply it, and safeguard it.[7] And today, there are many organizations that teach intuition among other personal skills.

We have put such an emphasis on intuition to indicate to the skeptics that an intuitive approach to thinking about the future and decision-making is not only valuable, but it really works.

Expect a Rebellion

As we mentioned earlier, some participants will want to jump to the end of the process—developing their vision and a detailed plan—before the end of the expansionary phase. Others get uncomfortable with some of the processes, as they are not used to using their imaginations and feelings in this way.

The process of changing mind-sets is not easy. Usually, it leads to a rebellion that takes place before lunch on the third day. We expect a rebellion, we warn leadership that it will happen, yet it can cause some concerns among the leadership. What they do not realize is that a rebellion indicates a positive turning point in the process, and we use it "for

---

6   Loran F. Nordgren et al., "The Best of Both Worlds: Integrating Conscious and Unconscious Thought Best Solves Complex Decisions," Journal of Experimental Social Psychology, March 2011, Pages 509–511.

7   Gary Klein, *The Power of Intuition,* Currency, Doubleday, 2003.

effect," rather than trying to defuse it. In many cases, we would have been disappointed if it had not happened.

One case in point was a rebellion in a workshop for a high-tech organization. On the morning of the third day, we were making a presentation on low probability but potentially high-impact events. Rebellions can be triggered by many different events that may appear to have little to do with the changing of mind-sets, yet that is what lies behind almost all of them. In this case, despite the fact that we said the events were very low probability and we were not trying to convince anyone that they were about to happen, the organization's chief scientist objected. He started to shout "b******t!" When his colleagues told him to "shut up!" he got louder, stood up, waved his arms, and walked right up to the presenter, who was a serious engineer himself. We all expected him to hit the presenter, but the presenter stood his ground. For a few seconds, perhaps even a minute, they stood nose-to-nose. Eventually, the chief scientist turned around and went back to his seat, without saying another word. Our colleague resumed the presentation. Later in the day, as the chief scientist began to understand more about what we were trying to do, he and the presenter became the best of friends.

Techniques for Phase 1

The techniques listed below and later described in detail in Chapter 9 are only some of those we use, but they are the ones we use most often, and generally in the order listed, although we intersperse the semi-analytical techniques with the creative ones. Over the years, we have developed many different techniques that we apply in specific circumstances. Sometimes we develop new methods "on the spot" based on our intuitive understanding of what is needed. This is the imaginative and creative phase for us as well as our clients, so there are no hard-and-fast rules.

Semi-Analytical Techniques Requiring Subjective Judgment

- Critical Issues and Dilemmas
- "Unmentionables"
- Energy Centers
- Mind-Map[8]
- Pinwheel: Assessment of Capabilities
- Reframing
- Identifying the Essence
- BCG Matrix
- Development Curves
- Nth Order Effects

Intuitive/Creative Techniques

- Teamwork: Guided Imagination
- Futuristic Guided Imagination
- The Metaphor
- The "Ideal If"
- Science Fiction
- Wild (Low-Probability/High-Impact) Ideas
- Advice to the Vision Makers—Brief Synthesis

Outline Agenda of a Typical Three-Day Expansion Session

The times given assume a total group of about 25 people and generally 4-5 small groups.

---

8   Mind-mapping was developed by Tony Buzan more than 30 years ago as a way to encourage the nonlinear development of ideas. His first book that included the subject was: *Use Both Sides of Your Brain,* Plume/Penguin, NY, 1991.

Day 1: Groundwork

Time	Activity	Mode
0830	Welcome, introductions	Plenary (P)
0900	Introduction to the workshop process, objectives	P
0930	Ground rules, Q/A	P
1000	BREAK	
1020	Hopes, fears, expectations for the whole VBP	Small Groups (S)
1040	Critical issues—share, discuss, prioritize	S
1110	Core dilemmas—share, discuss, prioritize	S
1145	Outbriefs, discussions	P
1230	LUNCH	
1330	Review highlights of interview material (on wall and in handouts)	Individual (I)
1350	Make notes of items that stand out	I
1400	Mind-map—trends that affect the future of the organization	P
1445	Thoughts on trends—prioritize with dots	P / I
1500	Identify key areas from mind-map that will become Energy Centers	P
1530	Break	
1550	Vote with feet to preferred Energy Center (reallocate people if uneven)	P
1600	Mind-map Energy Centers—be comprehensive	S
1700	Outbriefs on Energy Center work—discussion	P
1745	END OF DAY	

Day 2: All Expansion

Time	Activity	Mode
0815	Review WarRoom of previous day's work	I
0835	Introduction for day	P
0845	Wild Ideas from Sci-Fi/Fantasy—prioritize	S
0915	Attributes of top 5 ideas—what do we have today that is close?	S
0945	Implications of top 5 ideas for organization	S
1010	BREAK	
1030	Outbriefs on Wild Ideas work—discussion	P
1115	Implications for Energy Centers (EC)	ECs
1200	LUNCH	
1300	Metaphor—the organization of 2025 is like?	2 Groups
1345	2 Outbriefs	P
1405	Ideal If—it would be ideal for the organization of 2025 if…	S
1445	Break	
1505	Outbriefs on Ideal If work	P
1545	Implications for ECs—identify key capabilities required	ECs
1645	Walking review of ECs—everyone looks at all of them	I
1715	Plenary feedback on day, Q/A	P
1745	END OF DAY	

Note: Overnight we prepare a pinwheel from the key capabilities required.

Day 3: Some Expansion and Pulling Together

0815	Review WarRoom of previous day's work	I
0835	Introduction for day	P
0845	Place dots on Pinwheel	I
0915	Analysis by observation of Pinwheel—what's this telling us?	P
0945	Pinwheel—what's missing?	P
1000	BREAK	
1020	Implications of Pinwheel analysis for ECs— what capabilities are needed?	ECs
1050	Potential blocks and bridges to future capabilities	ECs
1120	Prep of outbriefs on all the important ideas emerging from the ECs	ECs
1200	LUNCH	
1300	Outbriefs	P
1400	Pulling the ECs together: What's this telling us about the future of the organization?	P
1500	BREAK	
1520	What kinds of things need to be done to ensure future success?	ECs
1550	Top 5 pieces of advice to the vision-makers	ECs
1610	Outbriefs	P
1645	Final remarks for this workshop, Q/A	P
1715	END OF FIRST WORKSHOP	

Note that the techniques selected for these three days are typical, but they do not cover the totality of the techniques we use. Sometimes we use Futuristic Guided Imagination instead of Sci-fi/Fantasy, as it takes a little less time. Sometimes we substitute a BCG Matrix for the Pinwheel, if we want to include a greater emphasis on innovation. All these techniques are discussed in detail in Chapter 9.

The final point to be made is that all the participants require some closure at the end of the three-day Expansionary Workshop. In the above agenda, you will see 1550: Top 5 pieces of advice to the vision makers. We ask the participants: "If you are not going to be present for the Synthesis Workshop, what advice would you want to make sure the vision makers have?" They work on this in small groups, prioritize their top 5 pieces of advice, and brief their results to the rest of the group. This advice becomes one of the key inputs for the Synthesis Workshop.

Key Points from this Chapter

■ This is the most critical part of the whole VBP process. It must be given time despite possible objections by "left-brained" participants.

■ There is usually a rebellion on the morning of the third day. Don't worry about it. It's part of the process.

■ By the end of Phase 1, the participants will have been through a creative and semi-analytical expansion and exploration of:

  • The strategic context of their organization.
  • Issues, concerns, and problems of the organization today and into the future.
  • Possible/potential desired directions.

■ By the end of this phase, participants will also have an example of a template for designing such an expansionary workshop for themselves, should they wish to conduct another one in a year or two.

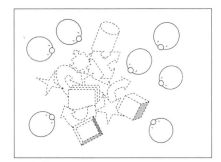

CHAPTER 9

VBP Workshop Tools and Techniques

Basic Principles

In this chapter, we start with a few basic principles of how we organize and conduct the workshops and then expand on the specific techniques for Phase 1 that we listed in Chapter 8. These are the techniques we use most often in this Expansionary Phase, *and they are listed in approximately the order in which we usually use them.* However, as we stated in Chapter 8, we frequently intersperse the semi-analytical techniques with the creative ones. The selection of the specific techniques is dependent on the particular problems and concerns faced by you and your organization. We illustrate the use of these techniques with specific examples. There are no hard-and-fast rules here about which techniques to use and how. It's a mix of common sense (asking yourself, "What do I really want to get out of this session?") and intuition.

Worksheets

As mentioned in Chapter 6 for all our small group sessions, we use specially developed and tailored worksheets. We have found that top-level executives work better when they have control over their own time and when they are able to work in their own way.

With worksheets, we specify the desired outcome for a particular session, give them a time by which they must be finished with the entire worksheet as well as the time allotted for each part, and make suggestions about how they might break the problem down. Examples of two typical worksheets are given below.

WORKSHEET – DATE

Worksheet 1 – Critical Issues

Color Groups

Select a timekeeper, a recorder and a presenter.

The purpose of this session is to discuss the 3 issues critical for the development of your organization that you brought with you as homework.

1200 – 1245

1200 (15 mins) Each of you, individually, take no more than 2 minutes to read to the others your 3 critical issues.

As the first person reads out his issues, *Recorder,* write them on a flip chart. When the next person reads his, write those down too, unless he has one that is similar to one of those identified by the first person. In which case, put an asterisk by that issue.

1215 (25 mins) As a group, discuss these issues in some detail amongst yourselves, and prioritize them. *You might start out by asking why is this issue important? Is it a root cause , or is there something more important behind it? Try to get to the root cause.*

1240 (5 mins) Write up the Top 5 critical issues on a separate flip chart and hand it to us.

Be prepared for a briefing at 1335, immediately after lunch.

Recorder, please make sure that the remaining flip charts are labeled correctly with Group Color, Worksheet Number, Title (Critical Issues) and Page Numbers. Then staple all of them together.

Figure 9-1: Worksheet Example

Figure 9-2: Worksheet Example

Small Groups

For our workshops, we generally develop several different sets of small groups from the known list of participants. This ensures that over the course of the workshop, each person gets to work with everyone on the team, ideally more than once and on different elements. As discussed earlier, this reinforces the team building and strengthens the overall consensus and team ownership of the workshop results.

We also ask the participants to "self-regulate" when they are in the small groups to ensure that everyone has the opportunity to be a recorder and presenter. This prevents one or two opinionated people from taking the lead too often and biasing the output, and it ensures that everyone has "air time."

For each set of small groups, we develop group names and group logos, which are posted in the area where each group will be working. Examples of such group names and logos include numbers, shapes, numbered shapes, letters, colors, or names of elements in various categories.

Adding colorful names and logos to the small groups adds to the participants' sense of group identity. The group names and logos are also posted on group rosters and in the WarRoom, where workshop results are displayed as we progress through the workshop.

Typical examples of small group logos, using numbers and shapes are shown in Figure 9-3.

Warrior Groups

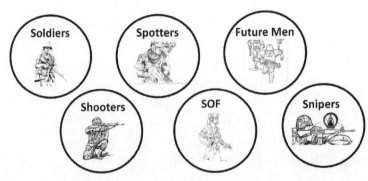

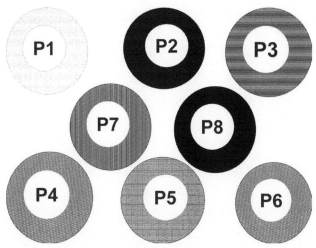

Figure 9-3: Examples of Small Group Identifiers

Ground Rules

In each workshop, regardless of the focus, we employ some basic ground rules that apply to how we work and how participants should interact with each other.

Our ground rules for small groups generally include the following:

- Speak for yourself, in the first person.

- Only one person should be speaking at a time; all others should be listening.

- When recording ideas, do not "filter" or edit other's ideas.

- Share in the decisions of the group.

- Value others' thoughts and contributions—actively listen.

- Allow space for others' views.

- Challenge behavior that inhibits the workshop.

- Challenge and criticize ideas, not people.

- Acknowledge that not all questions can be answered here.

- Record *unanswered questions* and *great, but not relevant ideas* in the "parking lot" and move on.

- Within each small group participants should take a role.

  We have an additional ground rule for plenary sessions:

- Only one person may speak at a time.
  - Do not hold conversations in the background, competing with the recognized speaker. It is rude and decreases the efficiency of the communications across your team.
  - No cellphones are allowed in the workshop—not even on vibrate.

Parking Lot

The "parking lot" referred to in the ground rules is generally a simple poster, placed near the WarRoom elements, where Post-It notes recording *unanswered questions* and *great, but not relevant ideas* are located. All these should be revisited from time to time in the course of the workshop, since they often become relevant later in the process. Some may be saved for review beyond the workshop. (See Figure 9-4 for some typical parking lot setups.)

Parking Lots

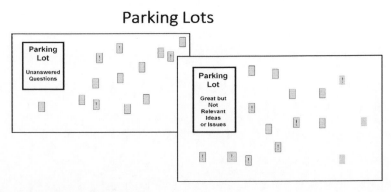

Figure 9-4: Typical Parking Lots

Active Listening

A technique we discuss in our introduction to each workshop is the notion of active listening. We encourage each participant to practice this throughout the whole workshop. What it means is, when another person in your group is speaking, *really* listen. Do not be thinking of what you are going to say next; really try to understand what the person is saying. Allow space in your mind for the views of the others in your small group.

Active listening visibly shows respect for each other and helps ensure that each participant has a say. It has been our experience that the deliberate practice of active listening increases the quality (and data rate) of the communications within the small groups.

WarRoom

The WarRoom, as we have developed it, is a way to capture visually all that happens in the workshop, from beginning to end. It is begun with initial entries that include workshop ground rules and objectives, and small group names and personnel assignments.

As the workshop progresses, the results of each session are collected and transcribed into PowerPoint format so they can then be printed in poster-sized format and posted on a wall selected for the WarRoom display. The WarRoom grows continually throughout the course of the workshop, allowing each participant to see when information and ideas were originated, by whom, and what that implied for succeeding sessions. As the WarRoom grows, the participants can visualize and internalize the work of the group as a whole, and often get new insights and ideas as a result of what they see.

The WarRoom will include all the diagrams they work on, such as Energy Centers, Mind-Maps, Pinwheels, and other "visuals" and templates that contribute to the development of the final products, including the Vision, Values, and Top-Level Objectives.

At the end of the workshop, the WarRoom provides a complete, sequential record of all they have done together and is an excellent tool for participants not only to remember and reinforce their sense of ownership and passions in the results but also to share these feelings with others in their organization.

Figure 9-5: Part of a WarRoom

Sometimes our clients will take parts (and on one occasion, everything) of the WarRoom and will stick them on a corridor wall or in the boardroom so that leadership can refer to it when they need to make future decisions. Those clients that have done this have found it to be very valuable, as it is always there for reference. We have started to recommend this.

Semi-Analytical Techniques Requiring Subjective Judgment

These are techniques that are often based on both analysis/data and subjective judgment. They are generally used to assess the magnitude of issues of concern to the participants, or dilemmas facing their organization for which there has been no detailed analysis performed. We either ask the participants to prioritize the importance or urgency of the concern or issue under consideration, or to rate it on a scale of 1-10 or 1-100.

Critical Issues and Dilemmas

For the first day of their workshop, we ask all participants to bring, in writing, three issues that they personally believe are critical for the future of the organization and one major dilemma facing the organization. We define a dilemma as a decision that you or someone in the organization must make that will result in only less-than-satisfactory outcomes.

Working in small groups, the participants discuss their issues and dilemmas, collate them as appropriate and prioritize them. Each small group presents its top three issues and dilemmas to the rest of the participants. Then they are collected and put on the wall in the WarRoom.

"Unmentionables"

We use the term "unmentionable" to describe an idea or thought that, if brought up in a meeting of the organization's leadership, would cause the person expressing the idea or thought to be admonished and expelled immediately from the meeting—or worse. Unmentionables generally evoke strong responses and feelings within the organization's leadership. The value of unmentionables is that they often expose serious, yet unstated, problems within the organization, and therefore must be dealt with as new visions, values, and strategic plans are developed.

This exercise is not always a part of our process. However, if we think that the organization has problems that are too difficult to discuss openly (as learned during the interview process), we add a session where we can work through their unmentionables.

Each person is asked to write on a 3x5 card significant problems they believe are crucial for the organization to solve for its future success.

These are the kinds of problems or views mentioned above that, if expressed out loud, could result in the people who identify them being fired, admonished, disciplined, etc. We collect the cards, type them in a very large typeface, cut them into strips, and ask participants to collate them under the following headings:

- Problems we can solve easily
- Problems we can solve, although not easily
- Problems that are completely beyond our control (including who needs to be consulted to solve each one).

Note: Once the problems on the 3x5 cards are typed up, we destroy the original cards so that handwriting cannot be identified.

We add the unmentionables to the WarRoom wall as additional issues to be addressed. By placing them on public view, participants have a chance to reflect on them and consider their potential solutions during the workshop.

Energy Centers

This is a technique we use fairly frequently. Energy Centers are filters through which the participants are asked to look at the organization throughout the rest of the workshop. These "filters" may come from reframing the nature of the organization's business or from a discussion of the issues and particularly the dilemmas. They are so-called because we want the participants to focus on the one they feel the most passionate about and into which they are willing to put a lot of energy. Once the participants have decided on energy centers and have given them names, we post them at intervals around the room. Then we ask the participants to walk to the one on which they want to work. If there is an imbalance, we ask for volunteers to move so the centers have approximately equal numbers of participants. We also ask for one person to volunteer to champion each Energy Center—to plead for it and its importance to the organization.

We ensure that the Energy Centers cover a wide range of the organization's business so that, together, the different perspectives are quite comprehensive. We then ask each group to flesh out its energy center using the Mind-Mapping technique described below. They return to the Energy Centers to continue to flesh them out after working on other sessions. (See Figure 9-6 for examples of Energy Centers from three different organizations.)

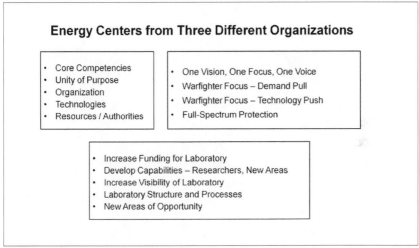

Energy Centers from Three Different Organizations

- Core Competencies
- Unity of Purpose
- Organization
- Technologies
- Resources / Authorities

- One Vision, One Focus, One Voice
- Warfighter Focus – Demand Pull
- Warfighter Focus – Technology Push
- Full-Spectrum Protection

- Increase Funding for Laboratory
- Develop Capabilities – Researchers, New Areas
- Increase Visibility of Laboratory
- Laboratory Structure and Processes
- New Areas of Opportunity

Figure 9-6: Energy Center Examples

Mind-Map[9]

A Mind-Map is a diagram used to depict and organize information about a subject. The subject can be an organization, a concept, an Energy Center, or even a meeting. We are usually interested in a Mind-Map of the client's organization, or its ideas for a new organization. To create a Mind-Map, we use a very large sheet of paper (consisting of 9 to 12 sheets of flip charts stuck together) with the subject of the workshop in the middle. This subject in the middle is often the "organization today" or the problem we are looking to solve. It can also be an Energy Center topic, as described above. The branches represent aspects of the organization and its operating environment, and we want it to be as com-

---

9   Tony Buzan, op cit

prehensive as possible. (Figure 9-7 shows a photograph of an original Mind-Map drawn during a workshop.)

We use the Mind-Map to enable the participants to share their different perceptions on the organization or topic. Frequently people from different parts of the organization see it from very different perspectives, so the Mind-Map serves two purposes. The first is that it provides a comprehensive view of the organization or topic, and the second is that, sometimes for the first time, people see aspects of the business they had never seen or understood before.

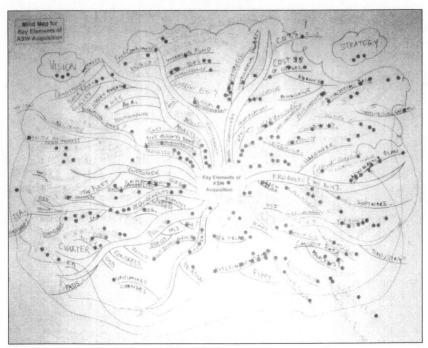

Figure 9-7: Photograph of a Mind-Map

Three people from our team start the mapping process—two with colored pens in hand and the third moderating the ideas flow. If we are looking at the current view of the organization, we ask the participants to call out what they see as the main parts of the organization. They can choose to see it from the perspective of divisions, functions, or technologies. As they call out the main parts, the two pen holders start to draw them in as branches. We ask the group first for the large branches, and then for the smaller ones, asking the participants who make the suggestions to tell us exactly where to put them. Sometimes the branches are the main areas that together form a comprehensive description of the organization or topic or, if we are doing a very future-oriented project, we may ask for areas that are experiencing significant change that might affect the organization or topic.

After doing this for about 45 minutes, we ask the participants to continue fleshing out the Mind-Map during their breaks, and other spare time. We also ask them to indicate links between branches so we can all see the relationship between the various branches and sub-branches. Late the following day, we give each participant 15 to 20 colored dots, and ask them to stick them on the most important branches. This mindmap is left on the wall as part of the WarRoom for the entire workshop. Occasionally, after reviewing the Mind-Map, the participants will redraw it in order to place greater emphasis on certain branches. If that is their preferred version, then that's the one that is kept.

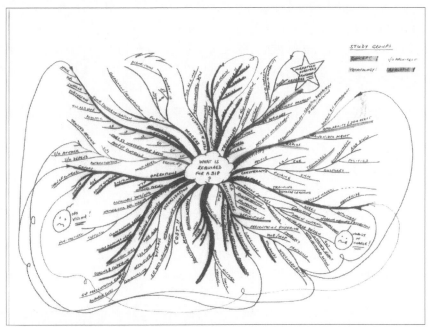

Figure 9-8: Redrawn Mind-Map Example

For the final report at the conclusion of the workshop, we redraw the Mind-Map, like the one shown in Figure 9-8. There are software programs for drawing Mind-Maps, but we prefer to do them by hand in order to replicate faithfully what the group has done. We have been told that people remember not only what is on the Mind-Map, but also the conversations that took place around it when it is copied this way.

Pinwheel: Assessment of Organizational Capabilities

This technique is used to provide a rapid assessment of the organization's technologies, systems, disciplines, intellectual and psychological capabilities, and more. It provides a qualitative measure and is based on the perception and knowledge of the participants. However, because there is the possibility for questioning, it can be very powerful. The specific technologies, capabilities, and the other elements become spokes of the Pinwheel. Participants are given colored dots—to stick on each spoke on the pinwheel—and are asked to rate every capability, element, or attribute from excellent to nonexistent (or "not a clue"). If there are polarized groups of dots, we ask the participants for reasons why some thought it was excellent and others poor. It is frequently because one part of the organization does not know what is going on in another part. A former Undersecretary of the Navy said that without this session, which took about 45 minutes, he would have spent at least 100 hours of his own time eliciting the same information. Once completed, the Pinwheel is left on the wall for the entire workshop.

In the Pinwheel in Figure 9-9, there are different colored dots that were put onto the diagram two years apart. The intent was to see in which areas the capabilities had improved and in which they had declined. We have also used different colored dots to indicate the part of the organization from which the participants have come. In one case, we used three colors—one for R&D, one for marketing, and one for finance. It was very instructive to see the differences in perception from those various groups.

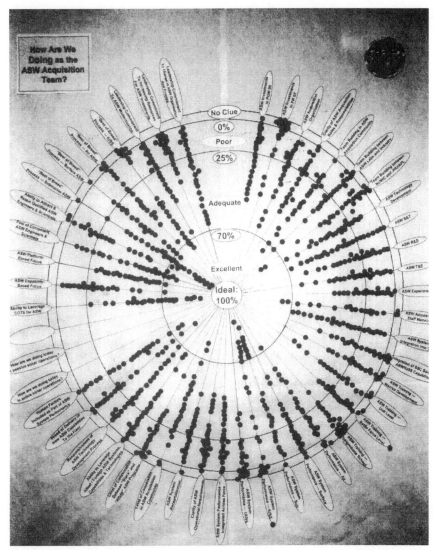

Figure 9-9: Pinwheel Measuring Qualitative Factors

Figure 9-10: Blank Pinwheel Example

Teamwork: Guided Imagination

Depending on our assessment of the group—how creative and open-minded they are—we may conduct several short Guided Imagination sessions. Guided Imagery is a technique used by a lot of athletes to practice moves and plays in their imagination. There's a well-known story about Olympic track and field athlete Carl Lewis, whose manager found him lying in a hammock apparently asleep. His manager asked him why he wasn't practicing. Lewis replied that he was—in his head. This wasn't too convincing for his manager, who then asked if he could help with anything. Lewis responded by asking him to move a stick a few feet further down the garden. Lewis looked at it carefully and then went back to his imagining.

We have a particular Guided Imagination technique that we use to get people to remember times when they have been on a really successful team. We ask about the team's characteristics and its leader. We get them to recreate the feeling of being successful, and then we ask them to bring those feelings into the workshop.

Guided Imagery works best if the leader/speaker has a soft, clear voice with good intonation. Try it yourself. Sit in a comfortable chair, and read aloud the following sentences in a soft, clear voice. Imagine yourself in the place of your audience, or try it on your spouse and children!

- *Close your eyes. Sit back and get comfortable.*
- *Recall a time when you were part of a successful, winning team.*
- *This could have been a sports team at school, a debating team, or it could have been a team working on an important project.*
- *Recall the team in detail—the team leader, each member. Recall their faces, the way they dressed, the way they talked.*
- *Recall a time your team was really successful. What did you do? High five each other? Jump up and down? Pat each other on the back and congratulate each other?*
- *See it, hear it, feel it.*
- *How did it feel to be part of that winning team? How did you feel?*
- *Bring that feeling into your mind and your heart. Breathe it in.*
- *And when you have it, open your eyes.*

When everyone's eyes are open, ask the following questions, and let two or three members of the group answer each one:

- What did it feel like to be on that winning team?
- What kind of a leader did you have?
- How did your special, winning team work?

Then tell the group to bring the feeling of that winning team into the work they are about to do. This helps them become more passionate, enthusiastic, and creative.

This is the imagery we use. When you use this technique, you should develop your own guided imagery that fits with your style and that of the group.

Futuristic Guided Imagination

We use this technique when we want the participants to build a shared perspective about some aspect of the future. We start the process of Guided Imagery by setting the scene, and then we ask for the picture to be fleshed out and expanded by having the participants contribute ideas and comments. We may ask for the group to visit someone, and we ask them to describe the scene in detail. For instance, "This is the year 2040, and we are visiting the CEO of Corporation X in his office. Where is his office? What does it look like from the outside? We go in through the main entrance—what do we see, hear, feel, smell? If his office is on the top floor, how do we get there (elevator or "Beam me up, Scottie?). Do we walk, or are there some form of walkways? What does the door look like? Do you knock and turn a knob or handle, or does it open on your approach? What does the office look like inside? What sorts of technology do you see?"

One of our clients used this kind of technique to think about developing an entirely new form of glass that could transform from transparent to opaque, and change color. Another client had the idea to use essential oils in the office to keep people bright and alert. Again, this is one of the techniques where we want people to use all their senses. Another one we have used frequently, for high-tech organizations, is to get the group to "go" to a warehouse where all the latest products for the year 2025 are stored and to walk through the aisles and tell us what they see, hear, smell, and feel.

Reframing

There are several definitions of Reframing. In this context it is a technique that refers to a frame of reference: internal (beliefs, values) or external (rules, policies). It is the process of seeing, hearing, or feeling the object, situation, or circumstance differently—from different perspectives, through different lenses. There are several types of reframing:

- *Image/Visual:* seeing material objects, landscapes, events, processes and even organizations and systems from different perspectives.

- *Linguistic:* using different words to describe the same thing, person, place.

- *Internal dialogue:* "talking to yourself" about circumstances, people, or events in order to develop a different understanding of them.

- *Feeling:* using a combination of talking and feeling to change *your* feeling about a circumstance, person, or event.

Figure 9-11: Wife and Mother-in-Law Illusion

In the Figure 9-11, we see an example of image reframing. Some people see a beautiful young woman, while others see an old hag. If you focus on one of the images, it is almost impossible to see the other. Only a very few people can see both at the same time. It is known as *Wife and Mother-in-Law,* and was published by W.E. Hill in 1915, although he acknowledged that it derived from an earlier German cartoon.

The reason that this is an important concept is that, very often, we see something so clearly that there is no doubt in our mind that we know exactly what it is, what it looks like, where it came from. We focus on it so intently that, when someone else sees something different, we think they are crazy. We think they just don't "get it," whereas *we* may be the ones not getting it. Or one of us may be seeing a symptom of something rather than the underlying cause.

For instance, many years ago, a high-tech manufacturing plant began to experience increases in spoiled coveralls—tears, dirt that didn't wash off. The immediate thought was that there was a problem with the processes—that the machinery was faulty and people were getting their coveralls snagged on the equipment. Then a manager with a broader perspective began to wonder if there was something more to it. With some careful questioning, he discovered that the workforce was unhappy with some new rules that had been instituted, and their way of showing displeasure was to create this fairly minor, yet annoying problem. This was a combination of Visual and Feeling Reframing.

The Home of the Future Project

This project is an excellent example of the power of Reframing, and of a futures-oriented workshop[10] (that gave our clients many ideas for new products, services, technologies and businesses). Reframing can often open up many new possibilities and even new directions for businesses and concepts.

An example of linguistic Reframing is the difference between "house" and "home." Generally, if we think of a *house,* we think about its design, location, structure, and materials. But a *home* includes the idea of the people who inhabit it and the home-based activities in which they are involved. Will Rogers conveyed the idea very well when he said, "It takes a heap of livin' to make a house a home."

---

10 Sometimes our clients have wanted a limited perspective about some aspect of their future, rather than a complete strategic plan. This can be accomplished using future-oriented workshops on specific subjects.

In addition to vision-based planning, we sometimes conduct future-oriented projects in which we use workshops for both single and multiple clients. These are used to get the companies to think more broadly and futuristically about their products and services as a basis for developing strategies. In the mid-1980s, there had been a great deal of publicity given to the U.S. Smart House Project[11] in the UK and Europe, but many people in those countries viewed these "high-tech" houses with great skepticism. However, many companies liked the idea of thinking about future houses/homes because they saw the potential for new business. Several large organizations asked us if we could design and conduct a project that could help them develop new ideas for futuristic homes that would be more appealing to their potential customers. So in 1986, we conducted a multi-client UK/European project on the Home of the Future from a demand-led perspective, rather than the technology perspective of the American project. Participants included senior managers from organizations such as BICC, British Gas, British Telecom, Courtaulds, the Electricity Association, GEC, Honeywell, Imperial Chemical Industry (ICI), Ideal Standard, Laing Homes, Marley, MK Electric, Pilkington Bros Ltd., Square D, TSB Group, and Unilever.

In the workshop, we first reframed the house into a home. Then we focused on what a home is for. Why do people want a home? What kinds of activities do they conduct in a home? We then organized those home-oriented activities into leisure, work, and maintenance. For instance, breakfast was considered *maintenance,* while having friends by for dinner was *leisure.* Figure 9-12 shows a schematic of the three broad activity areas and some of the specific activities we included

---

11 This was a project developed by the National Association of Home Builders, its members and key partners, in 1985. It was focused primarily on Home automation

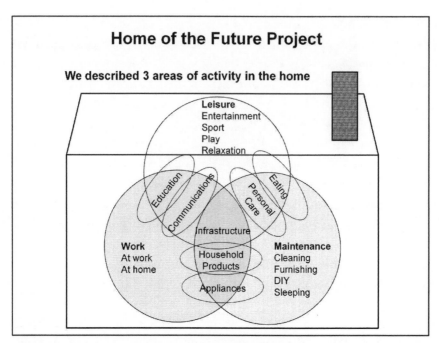

Figure 9-12: Home of the Future Project Elements

We also developed three scenarios based on people's values, since we knew that values underpin behavior and have a strong impact on what people want from a home. Sustenance driven (SD) people focus on security and belonging values; outer directed (OD) people focus on esteem values, and inner directed (ID) people focus on personal growth values. (For more information about values, see Appendix 1.) Figure 9-13 shows the three scenarios we used and the overlap between them. The overlap is important because those are the ideas that are common to all three scenarios—and are therefore likely to have a large potential market.

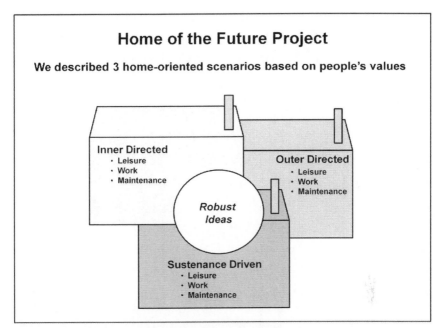

Home of the Future Project

We described 3 home-oriented scenarios based on people's values

Inner Directed
· Leisure
· Work
· Maintenance

Outer Directed
· Leisure
· Work
· Maintenance

Robust Ideas

Sustenance Driven
· Leisure
· Work
· Maintenance

Figure 9-13: Home of the Future Project Scenarios

In our workshops, we used Guided Imagery to picture the homes of people in various demographic groupings and especially in the values groups. In the workshops, we posed these questions to our senior management participants: What do SD people want in the way of leisure, work, and maintenance? Then we held a workshop on each of these broad activities. Finally, we asked: Given those wants and needs, what sort of home will SD people want? We repeated that format for the ODs and IDs.

It took some time, but it was worth it. The number of ideas that emerged blew the minds of the participants. They began to see the areas in which they were working in a new light. They began to question former assumptions. We had a very innovative architect working with us who never stopped asking the workshop participants questions of the "why?" or "why not?" variety. He drove many of them to distraction, but they came up with new ideas and ways of doing things that would never have happened without his questioning.

The group produced close to 8,000 ideas of which more than 2,000 were *robust* ideas for new products, services, materials, and technologies. Robust refers to the fact that these ideas were in the overlap area, common to the three very different scenarios. And 700 of these ideas cut across business sectors, so they would probably never have been identified by a single organization or sector. So the power of reframing, combined with workshops is enormous.

Future Capabilities Reframing

One of our clients already had a vision and strategic plan and wanted to know what capabilities its people needed for the future in order to achieve the vision. Typically in such projects, the organization thinks about what it's going to do in the future, what its operating environment might be like, what new technologies might be developed, and so on. This client's operating environment was so uncertain that the typical approach could result in so many possibilities and uncertainties that we advised against it. Instead, we suggested that they develop capabilities that would be of use to them in *any* future environment or circumstance. So we reframed their capabilities into the following three categories; the characteristics under each of the categories are just a few examples of what you could come up with.

Physical:

- Physical fitness, stamina, and endurance
- Understands and uses technology, but doesn't depend on it
- Performs in multiple physical environments – land, sea, air, jungle, desert…

Mental/Intellectual:

- Good communication skills
- Ability to think critically
- Ability to operate in ambiguous environments
- Ability to synthesize as well as analyze

Emotional/Psychological:

■ Ability to engage with others.

■ Patience/perseverance.

■ Awareness of their own strengths and limitations.

■ Integrity.

Altogether, we identified 10 to 15 capabilities or characteristics under each of the three headings. We put them all on a pinwheel and prioritized them. Then, working with our client, identified ways in which they might be taught or developed.

Identifying the Essence

Frequently an organization will be in many different businesses or have divisions that are very different in character. We first need to find its "Essence" in order to develop a vision and strategic plan for the *overall* organization.

Examples of Essence Diagrams

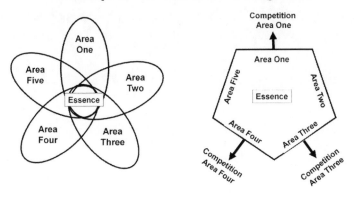

Figure 9-14: Generic Essence Diagrams

We generally use a simple diagram in which the various businesses or divisions and their respective activities are represented as "petals" around a center (a modified Venn diagram, if you will).

First, we ask the participants to write in each "petal" what they consider to be the Essence of a particular business, business area, or division. Then we ask them to think about the center—and what they regard as the Essence of the entire organization. That is indicated by the left-hand diagram in Figure 9-14.

Occasionally, an organization will have several business areas that seem to be defined by their competition. One client—a major retailer—defined itself that way, although the leadership did not consciously realize what it was doing. But it was clear from how the leadership spoke about its business that in four key areas they defined themselves by four different retailers whose sole business was one of those areas. The leadership did not seem to have any sense of what their own business was. We drew a polygon, such as the one shown in Figure 9-14, and put a question mark in the middle. It took some considerable time to get them to think through their real business areas and define them in a consistent, coherent fashion; but when they did, it opened many more opportunities. (To see actual Essence diagrams that were developed in the course of projects for two different clients, refer to Figures 9-15 and 9-16.)

The *Essence* of Retailer X

Purpose – To Provide Many Dimensions of Health and Well-being to Its Customers

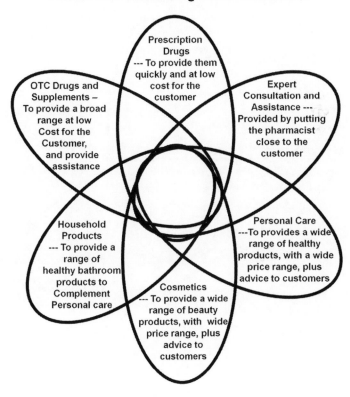

Figure 9-15: Actual Essence Diagram

Chief of Naval Education and Training
The *Essence* of CNET

Purpose -- To train and educate warriors and combat forces to conduct prompt and sustained Naval operations on and ... from the sea

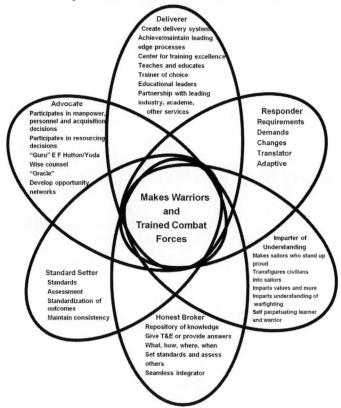

Figure 9-16: Actual Essence Diagram taken from the workshop WarRoom

STRATEGY WITH PASSION

The Metaphor

This technique is designed to get people to use their creative/intuitive capabilities. In fact, it is more than that. Each individual has a conscious mind and a subconscious or, more correctly, an unconscious mind. The conscious mind is the one we "use" most of the time. It is responsible for observing, analyzing, thinking, and rationalizing. The subconscious mind performs auto-pilot functions, such as breathing, and even motions related to driving an automobile. It also controls feelings and emotions and contains memory. It is this part of the mind that we "tap into" when we use this technique.

The technique is called Metaphor, although it is really a simile (we did not invent this technique or its name!). We facilitate this session with 15 to 20 people in each group. We make the statement: "The future of this organization is like…" and we ask the participants to call out anything that pops into their heads. It could be a word, a color, a song, a movie…anything, no matter how strange. We've had clients come up with such similes as pregnant salmon, Pink Floyd, sunrise, red balloon, bougainvillea, leaking ship, and Captain America. In other words, they will tell their colleagues that "The future of our organization is like a pregnant salmon!"

We then select the three most outrageous similes and unpack them by asking: "What are the characteristics of a …?" After doing this for all three similes, we ask: "What is this telling us about the organization?" The results are typically amazing, and the insights are always pertinent to the organization. For instance, *bougainvillea* has come up for several military organizations. When asked about the characteristics, the answers have been: When it has plenty of water, it produces lots of leaves and it grows, but it does not produce flowers. When it's suffering from lack of water, it produces flowers. In other words, according to the group's interpretation, declining budgets often trigger more creativity and invention. What's more, the participants have great fun doing this technique. There is always a lot of laughter, which breaks down barriers and creates a much more cohesive group.

The "Ideal If"

Following the Metaphor, we usually go into a small group session on the "Ideal If." Each group brainstorms to complete the thought: "It would be ideal for the future of this organization if…" Their answers may cover a very broad range of topics, from reorganizing to moving geographically or into new areas of business, or developing new technologies or products. In this session we may ask them to take a look at the Unmentionables and to incorporate ideas related to solving the problems expressed in that session into this one. When they have more than 30 ideas, we ask them to collate, discuss, and prioritize them. Since this is a brainstorming session, the ideas do not have to be relevant for, or achievable today. In fact, the more creative the ideas, the better.

Science Fiction and Wild
(Low Probability/High Impact) Ideas

Working in small groups, the participants bring in ideas from science fiction, fringe science, and fantasy. We ask them to identify ideas from books and movies that might be useful for the organization—in terms of new technologies, products, and services, or to give it an edge over its competitors. We want them to consider really wild ideas, and we push them to think out-of-the-box, and nothing is too wild or way-out. We have had all kinds of ideas emerge, from Romulan cloaking devices for the Navy SEALs, to telekinesis, mind-melding, zero-point energy, and controlling computers with your mind. We then ask questions about what kind of things we have or do currently that approximate the ideas; how could we achieve similar results in different ways. Sometimes we ask what would happen if we completely reversed the capability. To use the previous example, a Romulan cloaking device makes people invisible. We might reverse that and ask: "Would there be any benefit to being super-visible?" And that reverse questioning has led to some remarkably useful developments.

BCG Matrix

We sometimes use a modified version of the Boston Consulting Group Growth/Share Matrix to identify current and potential future capabilities. The original axes were "market growth and market share," and the four sections of the matrix were "stars," "cash cows," "question marks," and "dogs." We have many different sets of axes that we use depending on our clients' needs; for instance probability or difficulty of development and potential impact or effectiveness, value-added and priority, or cost and revenue. See Figure 9-17 for a generic matrix.

Working in small groups, we ask participants to place the current and potential capabilities in the matrix and ask them: "What would it take to move capabilities into either cash cows or stars?" Ideally, stars should be turned into cash cows as their novelty wears off, but sometimes they just fizzle and revert to dogs. Sometimes dogs—low value-added, low priority—are literally pet projects that belong to a member of the leadership, and it may be difficult to get them to abandon their pets. Woof! Question marks are frequently start-up projects that are believed to have star potential.

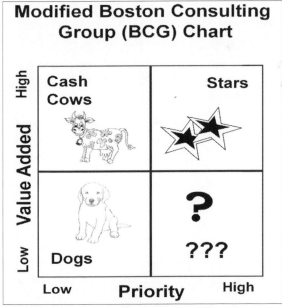

Figure 9-17: Generic BGC Matrix Chart

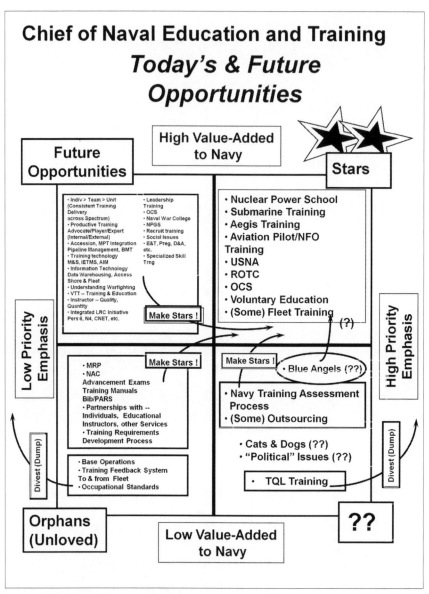

Figure 9-18: BGC Matrix Example

We used several versions of the BCG Matrix in a very successful project we conducted for the chief of naval education and training that led to the Navy's revolution in training. From 1998 to 2003, huge changes were made in how training was delivered, to whom, where and

STRATEGY WITH PASSION

what was included. One of the key intentions was to align enlisted and officer initial training programs under a single command structure. The example of the matrix in Figure 9-18 is just one of them.

Development Curves

If we need to assess the stage of development of some capability, technology, or system; or when we ask about what it would take to move a capability into a star, for instance, we draw an S-shaped curve on a flip chart. Then we ask the group to identify where they are on the curve—by sticking colored dots on it. We could get them to research the situation and provide "real" numbers, but the subjective assessment is actually more useful as it gets them to think more broadly about the nature of the development. We then pose a series of questions, first asking what is preventing them from moving up the curve. Then we ask what would help—more funds, people, other resources, fewer constraints? The diagrams in Figure 9-19 indicate the spread of responses, rather than showing the dots themselves.

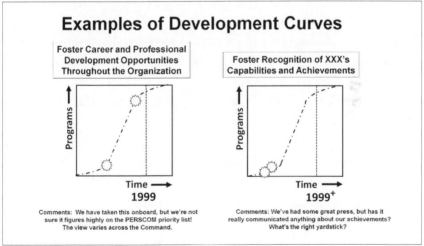

Figure 9-19: Development Curve Examples

Stakeholder Analysis

It is important to recognize all your stakeholders—the external as well as internal ones. These are all the people and businesses that interact with your organization, from the mailman to your best suppliers and customers; from your support "services to your shareholders. You need to identify your positive stakeholders—those who benefit from your success—and ensure you adopt approaches to keeping them that way. It is also useful to understand your negative stakeholders—those who are critical of your organization, or those who would benefit from your failure. While it is unlikely that you can win over the latter, you may do better with the former, if you pay attention to their criticism and develop some form of outreach. This is such an important subject that we address it in more detail in Chapter 11, "Communications Plan."

Nth Order Effects: Unanticipated Consequences

We have a combination of techniques for analyzing Nth order effects that include Mind-Maps and "What If?" scenarios. However, we also have a system of weighted matrices derived from decision impact analysis and cross-support analysis[12]. It was a technique designed to analyze the effects of making and implementing complex decisions that affect and are affected by a large number of factors. Although, at the time, computing power was limited, so modeling and simulation was not an option, there were benefits to be had by working through the impacts in person, and we still prefer to do it that way. Nth order effects are much more important than most people realize—that is where the idea of unanticipated consequences comes from – and why we still prefer to go through them with the decision makers involved. Most people are aware of first-order effects—generally the ones they want to achieve—and they may be aware of some second-order effects, which they refer to as potential downsides or upsides. However, there can be more. For instance, there was an agreement between the European Union (EU)

---

12 Christine A. Ralph (MacNulty) "The Beginnings of Cross-Support Analysis as Applied to the Fishing Industry" in Cetron and Ralph, *Industrial Applications of Technological Forecasting,* John Wiley & Sons, NY, 1971, pp274-289.

and the government of Tanzania to build a fish farm and processing plant at Mwanza at the southern edge of Lake Victoria. The first-order effect—Europeans get plenty of good fish and Tanzanians get jobs and money—appeared to be a marriage made in heaven. But the second- to fifth-order effects—highlighted in the documentary film *Darwin's Nightmare*—suggested nothing but disease, death, and destruction.

In Appendix 2, we continue our discussion of this disaster of imperfect planning and unanticipated consequences, and give a brief example of how we would have analyzed the decision to build the fish processing plant. This example provides a strong rationale for and insights into the value of considering possible adverse Nth order effects in your planning, even when it is difficult.

Key Points from this Chapter

- We have given you a wide range of techniques that we use most frequently in our Expansionary/Exploratory workshop to get participants to think creatively and out-of-the-box.

- We have given you creative, imaginative, and semi-analytical techniques, as well as specific examples of how and when we have used them.

- Play with these techniques and have fun; there are no right or wrong answers.

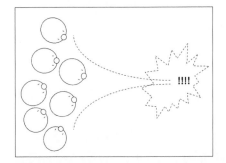

CHAPTER 10

Workshop, Phase 2: The Synthesis Phase

Focusing on the Future

The Phase 2 workshop requires the participants to pull together and synthesize all the material they produced in Phase 1 into a full VB Plan. Synthesizing is more than merely combining—it is the production of something that is more complex and different than the sum of parts. It is a new essence of what has gone before. It starts with the participants reviewing the WarRoom, which displays everything they did in Phase 1. It describes every major step in the process, and later, it provides a template for a typical Phase 1 workshop for the participants to use in the future. In the review, we ask them to focus especially on the Advice to Vision Makers, Mind-Map(s), the "Ideal If," and the Science-Fiction session. Next, we move to Steps 4-10, which are each designed to develop one element of the strategic plan.

Step 4: Develop the Vision and Values.

Step 5: Develop the Mission or Purpose.

Step 6: Develop Top-Level Strategic Goals.

Step 7: Develop Objectives to achieve goals.

Step 8: Develop strategies to achieve each Objective.

Step 9: Develop an Action Plan (measures, metrics, timeline, assign roles, and responsibilities).

Step 10: Develop an Implementation Plan (roles, responsibilities).

Step 11: Develop a Communication Plan.

We often create a diagram that illustrates how each workshop session (building block) contributes to the strategic plan as a whole. We will try to do the same thing in this chapter, discussing what each step involves and how it is essential to the development of the strategic plan.

Step 4: Develop the Vision and Values

A Vision provides direction for the organization, a guiding star, if you will. It is not quantitative, and it is not directly measurable; it needs to be futuristic or timeless.

Following are examples of actual Vision Statements:

- *Amazon:* Our vision is to be earth's most customer centric company; to build a place where people can come to find and discover anything they might want to buy online.

- *Mazda:* To create new value, excite, and delight our customers through the best automotive products and services.

- *Nike:* To be the number one athletic company in the world

We always develop a Vision from the perspective of either demand-pull or requirements-pull. In other words, we ask you to develop a vision for 5, 10, or 20 years into the future, from the perspective of what your customers or clients might want, or what you might be asked to do. Then we work backward to the present to see what it takes to make the demand-pull meet the supply-push or technology-push. It is not a linear process, and we frequently develop mini-scenarios to understand how they might make it work. Figure 10-1 illustrates this, with the squiggly lines representing this meeting process. Some organizations try to develop visions from technology-push perspectives, but these are generally less than successful, as they rarely take the end-user or consumer into account.

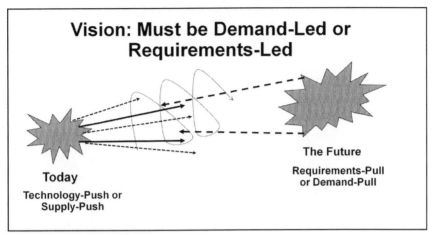

Figure 10-1: Vision Chart

Following the review of the WarRoom, the participants work in small groups, where each participant writes down in a notebook the five key elements they believe need to be in the vision. Then, one at a time, the participants write down these elements on flip charts. The first participant writes down all five elements. If the second participant has an element that is very similar to one that the first person wrote down, then they add a checkmark next to that element, and then write down the remainder of the list. This is repeated until everyone has listed or checked off all the elements. Then the group prioritizes the whole list.

Each small group then writes a vision statement that contains all or most of the high-priority elements. The groups bring up their flip-chart easels to the front of the room, stand them in a row, and then read their efforts aloud to all the participants. The participants discuss the ideas and then vote on their preferred vision statement, and we, the consultants, ask if there are parts of the rejected Vision Statements that people would like to add to the preferred one. This is usually done by giving each person three colored dots to stick on the various parts of the sentences.

Finally, two or three people are asked to volunteer to write the final draft Vision Statement. This gets posted on the wall, and left for 24 hours for comments, tweaks, and rewrites. We then go through a final version of the Vision and get agreement on it from all participants. We seek *consensus, not compromise,* and we will work until we get it.

Clarification of Critical Terms

- A *Vision* is what an organization will be or become. It is generally written using existential verbs.

- A *Vision* for a concept is what the concept will be or become. It is generally written using existential verbs.

- *Values* are deeply held beliefs that have a strong emotional component.

Values

Everyone has Values, even if most people are not aware of them. An organization's values need to be in alignment with those of its workforce. If they are not, then it can cause stress within the organization.

We put people into groups of three or four, and ask them to write down their Values on a 3x5 card. If people are not aware of their Values, we ask them to think about things that make them mad or make them really happy. Then we help them get to the root cause of their feeling. So, for instance, if people who are late for meetings makes the person mad, it's not just lack of punctuality that is the problem, the root cause is usually lack of respect for others. This means that one of the person's Values is *respect for others.* If seeing a movie in which someone triumphs over adversity makes a person feel happy or positive, then a likely value is *courage or perseverance.*

Once each person has written down four or five Values, we ask them to share them with the other members of their group, and also ask them to think about how they might play out in the organization.

Then we ask each small group to join with another one so we have groups of six to eight people, and we give them the task of developing Values for the organization. There are some organizations with a lot of history; the armed forces, for instance, where each service has had its own values for hundreds of years and is probably not going to change them. The same is true of other very old, and especially family-owned companies. In these situations, it is still useful to develop values that are appropriate and relevant for today, and individual commands can develop their own Values as well. We ask each group to produce six to eight Values and to think through how they might manifest in the organization. In other words, what does *respect for others* mean to a senior manager versus a person on a production line? For the senior manager, it might mean always being punctual. For someone on the production line who has to clock into his job, that is not an option, but it may mean making the place as clean and tidy as possible after a shift, or it may mean not cussing and swearing. Each group then presents its Values to the others, and we go through a process of collation similar to what we used to develop the vision statement. If some values have been identified by every group, then obviously those should be included in the final list. However, we still ask everyone to prioritize the Values by assigning colored dots (usually three per person).

Step 5: Develop the Mission or Purpose

Commercial organizations that are focused on products and services frequently have good, descriptive Mission Statements, yet they have no Vision. This is a mistake, as the two are very different concepts. Military organizations are assigned their Mission, although they may need to add to it or develop a separate statement of Purpose.

Following are some actual examples of Mission Statements:

- *Avon:* The Global Beauty Leader: We will build a unique portfolio of beauty and related brands, striving to surpass our competitors in quality, innovation and value; and elevating our image to become the beauty company most women turn to worldwide.

- *Chevron:* Providing energy products and services that are vital to society's quality of life.

- *McGraw-Hill:* To provide essential information and insight that help individuals, markets, and societies perform to their potential.

The process of developing a Mission Statement is identical to developing a Vision Statement, so please refer back to that section for instructions.

Clarification of Critical Terms

The *Mission* or *Purpose* is what the organization does or what it is for. It is described with action verbs.

Step 6: Develop Top-Level Strategic Goals

Top-Level Strategic Goals are those that define desired results that will enable the achievement of the organization's or concept's Vision and Mission. In our experience, there are usually between five and eight goals that, between them, cover all aspects of the organization and its business. If the organization has several divisions, there is sometimes a temptation to develop a major goal for each division. This temptation should be resisted, as it fosters stovepipes. Rather, the Top-Level Goals should relate to the overall organization's Vision and Mission. If we are developing a future concept, then the goals need to define all the major areas that must be worked on for the achievement of the concept. Ideally, they should be quantitative, but on occasion they may be too broad; in that case, they can provide a sense of direction. That is acceptable at this stage, although when we get to the next step—Objectives—we *must* have Measures and Metrics.

Following are examples of Top-Level Strategic Goals (from real clients' VBPs).

The examples in **bold** are the ones expanded on in subsequent stages of the analysis

- *Goal 1:* **By (date), develop and resource an integrated, end-to-end investment strategy to ensure an effective, efficient (particular technological) capability.**

- *Goal 3 (of 6):* Develop a Strategic Communication Plan to foster awareness of capabilities among all stakeholders by (date).

- *Goal 5 (of 5):* Establish a Research Center by (date) to develop new, relevant technologies for (specific future) Missions.

So once the participants have a Vision and a Mission, they need to think about the key things that must be done to achieve them. In other words, they need to agree upon the Top-Level Goals, that together comprise the Vision and Mission . In small groups, we ask all the participants to review and prioritize parts of the WarRoom, suggesting they focus on the following key areas:

- *Mind-Map,* especially the large branches. It is sometimes useful to give every member of the group 10 dots or checkmarks to place on the branches or sub-branches of the map they believe are most important. See how the dots/checkmarks cluster and what kinds of goals might be derived from them.

- *Energy Centers:* Could these be turned into goals?

- *Essence Diagrams:* What is in them that could be turned into goals?

- *Missing Areas:* What have we not covered? What's missing?

Continuing in small groups, participants ask themselves: If we achieve these goals, will we be able to achieve the Vision and Mission? If not, what needs to be added? Can any of the areas/goals be consolidated? Participants keep working through the goals until the group has a list of five to eight goals it likes and cover the organization's business or the concept we are working on.

Each small group then presents its set of goals to the others. Their flip charts are lined up in a row at the front of the room, and the whole group, plus the consultants, compare the various goals and conduct a first round of consolidation, pulling together goals that appear to be similar. Each participant is then given five colored dots and asked to prioritize the goals. If there is significant consensus on certain goals, then those goals move to the final list. If there are others that have emerged as possibilities, but without complete consensus, then we discuss them and eventually arrive at a small number of additional goals—generally from five to eight Top-Level Goals.

Again, we ask ourselves, "What's missing?" Can we achieve the Vision and Mission with these goals? Is there anything we need to add either to an existing goal or to make an additional goal? We have often found that "communications with internal and external stakeholders is missing from the main list of Top-Level Goals.

Outcomes

Although it may seem obvious, when we develop a goal or objective, we need to think through very carefully what exactly we are expecting the outcome of its achievement to be, what it will do for us, and what it will take to reach it. Very often, people confuse outcome with output, or even with performance, which can lead to misunderstandings. An outcome must be stated positively (we want to accomplish something, some result, or consequence), and it must be doable (no negative words or concepts, like avoiding or minimizing).

We then develop strategies to achieve the objective or goal, which include assigning responsibilities and developing a timeline by which it must be achieved. Of course, part of the strategy includes ensuring that the necessary resources will be available. It can also be useful to ask such questions as, what will and won't happen if we don't achieve the outcome?

Measures and Metrics

There are different definitions of *Measure* and *Metric*. We are using the most commonly accepted definitions. And we should note that you can have Measures and Metrics of both *effectiveness* (how well we are achieving an outcome) and *performance* (how well the process/system is performing)—you need both and should not confuse the two.

- A *Measure* generally has an element of human judgment. It is generally about the *what* that is to be measured.

- A *Metric* is an indicator or value that can be observed singly or collectively (e.g., time, length of turn, speed, distance, and other countable events). Metrics are directly measurable and generally form the answers related to the *how* and *how well* of outcome achievement or system performance.

Following are examples of Measures and Metrics:

- *Measure:* Task completion time.

- *Metrics:* Start and end time.

- *Measure:* Effectiveness of communication.

- *Metric:* Yes response.

- *Measure:* Efficiency.

- *Metrics:* Time, user ratings, tool usage, measures of system breakdown.

- *Measure:* Customer satisfaction.

- *Metrics:* Number of complaints, number of product returns, ratings in consumer satisfaction survey.

Step 7: Develop Objectives to Achieve Each Top-Level Goal

Depending on the number of Top-Level Goals and the number of participants, we may conduct this step in one or two rounds, as we need four to five people to work on each goal. We place the flip charts with each goal around the room, and ask the participants to "vote with their feet," by walking to the goal they want to work on. We recommend they go to a goal about which they feel passionately and also about which they know something.

Each small group then discusses its Top-Level Goal. The group can do this formally, by working through each bullet point in turn, or it can be done informally, taking the concepts and working through them in a less formal manner. To develop Objectives for each goal, participants follow four steps.

Step 1. State the outcome of the Top-Level Goal in the positive.

Step 2. Ensure the goal is doable by breaking it down into its main components, or Objectives.

Step 3. Ask how they will know when they have achieved the goal's outcome? *The answer to this question will help identify the Measures and Metrics for progress toward achievement of the goals.*

Step 4. Identify who will be responsible for the achievement of the goal, and who will be accountable.

Following are examples of Objectives, using **Goal 1** from the previous section:

- *Goal 1:* **Develop and resource an integrated, end-to-end investment strategy to ensure an effective, efficient capability.**
  - *Objectives for Goal 1:*
  1. Determine current efficiency/effectiveness within four weeks.
  2. Develop measures of value within four weeks.
  3. Develop improved method to measure effectiveness within eight weeks.
  4. **Change processes/resources based on demonstrated improvements; set up team to do this within four weeks.**
  5. Learn from industry in measuring business efficiency; meet with leaders from eight Fortune 500 companies within six weeks.
  6. Identify capability gaps (capabilities required to complete end-to-end capability that we don't yet have) within eight weeks.
  7. Partner/outsource with other businesses; develop plan within eight weeks.
  8. Foster personal growth, smart work, align needs of organization to needs of individual; develop plan to do this within eight weeks.

Once they have gone through this process with the Top-Level Goals, then the small group takes each Objective in turn and—with the exception of the additional two steps below—goes through the same process.

Additional Steps

Step 5. Where, when, with whom, and how do we want it to happen? And who else might be included? This assigns roles and responsibilities for the Objectives.

Step 6. What resources do we have to achieve the outcome, and what resources do we need to acquire?

Following are examples of Objective Components, using **Goal, 1 Objective 4** from the previous section. *Step 5* is embedded in each component as the person who is responsible for the Component:

- *Goal 1, Objective 4:* **Change processes/resources based on demonstrated improvements.** Components include:

   1. *VP Planning:* Propose org changes and identify subsequent cost related to establishing knowledge management (KM) structure as integral part of org. (date).

   2. *VP Finance:* Establish elaborated assessment process to assess effectiveness of knowledge sharing and creation processes and practices to include assessment of systems and policies (date).

   3. *Executive VP:* Set up Task Force to assess and promulgate lessons learned from Companies X, Y, Z (date).

   4. *VP Procurement:* Incorporate KM measurements and metrics as part of the procurement process (date).

   5. *VP Finance:* Assess and ensure resource changes to accomplish Goal 1 (date).

Step 8: Develop Strategies to Achieve Each Objective

By using this approach, the strategies become so obvious that they almost "fall out" of the previous step. The small group then takes the components of the Objectives from the previous task, and asks these questions:

- If we turn these components into strategies, will we have a comprehensive strategy for achieving the Objective?

- What other steps must be taken to achieve the Objective? Turn those steps into strategies.

- In what order do those strategies need to be accomplished?

- What are potential enablers? Who may be able to help and how? What additional resources might be useful?

- What are potential inhibitors? Do we have the skills and capabilities? Are there any policies in place that might inhibit us?

- Who should be responsible for each strategy?

Once these questions are answered, each group pulls together all the Objectives and strategies for each Top-Level Goal and presents it to the other groups. The whole group then discusses all the Top-Level Goals, objectives, and strategies, and any links, overlaps, or gaps between them. The consultants capture the discussion using a modified Mind-Map, and the group decides how to handle links and overlaps, and how to fill in the gaps.

Step 9: Develop the Action Plan

The Action Plan is a sequence of steps that must be taken or activities that must be performed well for a strategy to succeed. An action plan has three major elements:

- *Specific tasks:* What will be done and by whom?
- *Time horizon:* When will it be done?
- *Resource allocation:* What specific funds, hours, facilities, etc., are available for each activity?

The participants return to the small groups they were in for the previous session, and develop an action plan and timeline for all the steps that must be taken to achieve the strategies. The Action Plan is quantitative—in other words, it has something measurable that must be accomplished by a certain time in achieve the strategy. There may be several action steps for each strategy.

Each group is assigned a different color of Post-It notes. Once the group has developed its Action Plan, it writes down the major steps on the notes, and they are placed, in order, on a huge timeline we have prepared that covers the appropriate number of years. We then photograph the entire timeline.

Finally, all the participants take a first rough look at the timeline and comment on any obvious discrepancies in the timing of the tasks. This is another good time to ask "What's missing?" questions. Later, the organization's strategic planning group will prepare a proper critical path analysis of all the tasks.

Step 10: Develop the Implementation Plan

An Implementation Plan is also a sequence of steps, but it describes the *how*. It discusses in greater detail the responsibilities of those individuals accountable for overseeing the Action Plan. It also discusses policies and procedures, in case problems are encountered with the Action Plan. It often contains information on possible inhibitors and problems, and outlines ways to deal with them.

Creation of the Implementation Plan is generally the responsibility of the organization's Strategic Planning Group. If necessary, we recommend that organizations establish such a group before the workshops start, or at the very least, create one from among the participants. The Strategic Planning Group can also be responsible for tracking key issues—especially the STEEP ones—to ensure the organization does not miss any significant changes taking place.

Step 11: Develop the Communication Plan

Generally, the subject of a Communication Plan comes up as one of the Top-Level Goals. If it does, then we work with it there, as part of the overall strategic plan. If not, we add it at the end.

The example from earlier in this chapter is a fairly simple one, and we expand on it below.

- *Goal 3 (of 6):* **Develop a Strategic Communication Plan to foster awareness of capabilities among all stakeholders by (date).**

  - *Objectives for Goal 3*
  1. Identify key stakeholders and the roles they play by (date).

  2. Identify key supporters; plan to meet with them monthly starting (date).

  3. **Prepare Strategic Communication (SC) campaign plan by (date), including:**

     - Content, tone.
     - Media: electronic, written, display.
     - Obtain CEO/COO approval by (date).

- Launch first SC Campaign by (date).
- Start assessment process by (date).

- *Objective 3 for Goal 3: Director of Communications,* **Prepare SC campaign plan by (date).** Components include:

1. Establish SC Group by next Wednesday (12th) to develop this.

2. Discuss leadership week with the organization (17th–21st) to establish SC requirements and target audiences.

3. ID key stakeholders and contacts within three weeks.

4. Make contact with stakeholder contacts by end of week 4; discuss what they would like to see and what to expect.

5. Develop draft SC Campaign Plan by (date), including:
   a. Content, tone.
   b. Media: electronic, written, display.

6. Get Campaign Plan reviewed by leadership.

7. Go final with Campaign Plan by (date).

8. Execute Plan—details.

If it doesn't come up as a goal, we recommend that the organization develop a Communication Plan separate from the overall organizational strategy, as it is a critical element in getting all your stakeholders, including employees, to understand what your organization is and does. Refer to Chapter 11 for more on this subject.

Key Points from this Chapter

- In Phase 1, you, the leadership explore ideas and possibilities.

- In Phase 2, you synthesize all the material from Phase 1 into a coherent whole—a complete, Vision-Based Strategic Plan for the whole organization.

- This synthesis starts with the Vision, and cascades down through the Top-Level Goals to Objectives, Strategies, Actions and Implementation. Each of these elements is worked on in separate workshop sessions.

- It is useful to describe these elements as building blocks so everyone (leaders, managers and others) can see how they were developed and fit together.

- At the end of this session you will have the complete strategic plan.

PART IV:
What's Next?

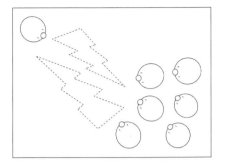

CHAPTER 11

The Importance of a Communications Plan

Communicate, communicate, communicate

The last step of Phase 2 is Step 11: Develop a Communication Plan. Whether this is accomplished as part of the overall VBP, as discussed in the last chapter, or whether it is developed separately, the purpose for it is the same. This chapter discusses what a communications plan needs to impart.

> "The problem with communication is the illusion that it has occurred." — *George Bernard Shaw* (1856-1950) Irish playwright and essayist

We communicate to inform, persuade, and influence people; to share ideas; to find out about things and people; and to socialize. And, most important from an organization's perspective, we also communicate to help change the organization's culture. This aspect of changing cultures is discussed separately in Chapter 12.

In this context, people need to know about the organization and its 6 W's+H --- What? Why? Where? When? Who? Who else? How? They need to be clear about what the organization is and does, how that might affect them, and what they might need to do with or for the organization. So the communications plan needs to be targeted to stakeholders both within and outside the organization.

There have been a number of studies recently that suggest that organization leadership is not doing a very good job of communicating with its stakeholders and employees. We hear a lot about the public's hostility to big business and Wall Street. But the problem is generally not hostility; it is a lack of understanding of what corporations (or government agencies or other large entities) are about. And it's not just outside the organization where there is lack of understanding; it's also within. There have been many studies showing that employees do not understand what their company does. The latter case is a failure of leadership—a failure of its ability to communicate. As specific examples, data from *2013 TINYpulse Employee Engagement Survey* indicated that only 42 percent of *employees* knew their organization's *Vision, Mission*, and *Values*. A recent survey for i4cp's annual *Critical Human Capital Issues* study indicated that 46 percent of high-performing companies and 83 percent of poor performing companies are not regularly communicating goal progress to their employees.

While a new Vision, Mission, Values, and Strategic Plan (VMVSP) must be communicated as quickly as possible, while the leadership is still fired up with enthusiasm, there are many other things to be communicated. Communicating to all stakeholders is an ongoing process—telling them good news as well as bad.

Good communication has many benefits, from improving morale, productivity, recruitment and retention of employees, to positive investor relations, general public support, government support, and better community relations.

Strategies to Win Acceptance by Internal Stakeholders

A Communications Plan is needed to share the VMVSP with the whole organization, affirming the support of the top leadership and infusing everyone with the passion generated by the leadership. This can sometimes be a daunting task, depending on the size of the organization and the receptivity of its employees.

An organization-wide presentation is often the best approach, with the leadership making presentations to the headquarters' staff and others. The presentations should be filmed and distributed to all parts of the organization. Rather than expecting people to look at it of their own volition, a member of the leadership should be there to explain what it means to the middle managers and other employees in terms they understand and are meaningful to them.

We have frequently found that middle managers are the most difficult people to convince. They've been in the organization long enough to say, "Been there, done that, many times before." They are often concerned that the new strategic plan will mean more work for them, because that has been the case in the past, and with no increase in salary or opportunities for advancement.

So the presentation of the VMVSP to the middle managers needs to incorporate honest assessments of what this will mean for them. What extra work will they be required to do? What might they be able to drop because of this new plan? But the key to their acceptance is to ask them what contributions (beyond the work that is required) they could make to achieve this plan and to find some means of rewarding them when they do so.

Presentations to the workforce should have a similar tone and objective. However, in this case, it is often very useful to speak to first-line supervisors and workers directly, and ask them to identify what they can to do to help achieve the new vision, mission, and goals, and to reward the teams for good ideas that are used by the organization.

In all cases, we need to think about the people to whom we are communicating. What do they know? What do they think they know? What do you think they know that is wrong? What do they believe? Without wishing to be condescending, we need to ensure we are using language and terminology they will understand. An understanding of their values (and your own) is often useful.[13] (Appendix 1 provides a basic understanding of values.) The words used should be related to their values and interests. For instance, people with values at the lower end of Maslow's Hierarchy of Needs tend to talk about family, home, and the desire for security. Those in the middle are more concerned with making money and gaining status and power, and those at the top end of Maslow's hierarchy prefer to talk about ideas.

Using the three methods of communication derived from Neuro-Linguistic Programming[14] —visual, auditory and kinesthetic—can also make a difference in the number of people who relate to what is being said. Visual people (the smallest group in the population) use and relate to visual words and cues (picture, sight, future), so when speaking with them they will resonate with comments such as: "Look how well your daughter is doing in school, she's smart and bright and clearly destined for big things!" Auditory people relate to auditory words (sound, loud, story), for instance: "I hear that your son is a great communicator and story-teller, and has a wonderful speaking voice." And kinesthetic types relate to words such as feeling, touching, sensing – "How did that pre-sentation grab you? It was so lively and uplifting!" The use of all these types of words in a speech or written communication ensures that the message resonates with more people.

Communicating the VMVSP to External Stakeholders

Communicating to external stakeholders is a form of diplomacy. An organization needs good relationships with the general public, share-holders, Wall Street, suppliers, customers, unions (if appropriate), and many more.

A new VMVSP needs to be communicated to external stakehold-ers just as quickly as to the workforce. They want to know what it will

---

13 Chris Rose, *What Makes People Tick,* Matador, UK, 2011.
14 Lewis & Pucelik, *The Magic of NLP Demystified,* 2d Ed., Crown House Publishing, UK, 2012

mean for the organization and its performance, and what it will mean for them.

One commercial client in the pulp-and-paper industry had a very difficult set of stakeholders, including a trade union, the government (in the form of policy constraints on both workforce and overseas customers), environmentalists, and some difficult and demanding clients. Once they had developed their VMVSP, they had to interpret it very carefully to their workforce and the different sets of stakeholders. This meant keeping the same words and sense as the VMVSP, but interpreting it in ways that made sense to each stakeholder. This required some very careful and sophisticated communications so people did not think they were telling different versions to different people. They had to be seen as honest and authentic. This was a difficult task, but they succeeded.

However, communications with external stakeholders also need to be ongoing. They frequently cover such topics as product and service quality, concern for both the consumers and workforce, financial strength, growth rate, breadth and depth of offerings, concern about the environment, and so on. If carried out well, communications can be part of a risk-management strategy and very effective in assisting with sales, recruitment, reputation, and more. But if done poorly, it can contribute to disasters.

A word of caution: New forms of social media are revolutionizing the way organizations interact with their stakeholders and vice versa. Make one misstep, one appearance of something being covered up, and the message will travel around the world in seconds. This may be a good thing, since it is ultimately likely to make organizations more honest and authentic, but until companies develop a greater understanding of what good communication requires, there may be problems and even crises. Being aware of what people are saying about your organization is a necessity, and having some prepared responses to crises will be very useful. Many large organizations already have public relations or strategic communications agencies collecting data on what is being said or written about the organization on a worldwide basis, and some conduct surveys of customers and other stakeholders. These agencies can also provide crisis communications, and they are experts at using social media. Some organizations have their internal departments that do all that. Provided the people in those departments are experts in social media and keep up with the latest developments, internal departments have the added advantage that they are there on the spot, aware of what is going on, and therefore able to respond immediately. Regardless, this is a function that is increasing in importance and needs to be included in an organization's capabilities.

Key Points from this Chapter

- Communicating your VBP to all your stakeholders is a critical and often overlooked part of your plan.

- Your internal stakeholders—employees—are more likely to work well if they know what the organization is about: its vision, mission and values.

- Your external stakeholders are likely to provide better service if they know how they fit in and what is expected of them.

- And clearly, you must communicate effectively with your shareholders in order to maintain their trust.

- The same, overall message needs to be communicated in ways that make sense to each different stakeholder, without compromising or diluting the real message.

- You need to be prepared to deal with negative messages that can be spread like wildfire through social media.

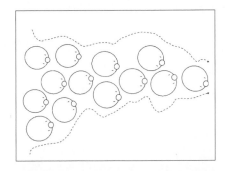

CHAPTER 12

Changing Cultures—
Critical for Success

"If we continue to do what we've always done, we'll continue to get what we've always got." — *Henry Ford*

In these times of increasingly fast-paced change in the world in general, we find that some organizations seem to have blinkers on. When the leadership team takes a day or two to think about the future of the organization, we often hear people say, "Oh, it's all very well for the leadership to have these off-sites and to come up with some new vision, but what's going to happen once they get back to their offices? Nothing's going to change."

We are not advocating change for change's sake. And we want to mention that change and transformation are not synonymous. Transformation is an organizational event that is big, bold and can be risky. If it's done well, it can make a huge difference to an organization's success, and it will include change. It can be driven by a new Vision, Mission, and Strategic Plan, and it *is* going to require some change. But change does not include transformation. Change is usually limited in scope, clearly defined and with a desired outcome in mind. Change is also not reorganization, although it may require some of it. This chapter presents an approach that has been used in many commercial and government organizations. It recognizes that organizational and cultural change starts with people. Thus the key is to create cultural change by getting employees aligned with the Vision and Mission, then creating the appropriate strategies to achieve them. It focuses on the people who comprise an organization, rather than on the setting in which they function.

Cultural Change Following Mergers and Acquisitions

Cultural change is particularly important following a merger or acquisition, when the leadership wants to form a single entity from two very different ones. Most mergers and acquisitions are made for financial or market reasons, with little emphasis placed on the effect the move will have on the people and cultures of the merging organizations. Many mergers and acquisitions fail or do not meet the leaderships' expectations of performance because the people and cultures were not taken into account. One exception to this is Procter & Gamble. The former chairman, Robert McDonald, told us that, when considering an acquisition, they spend more than two years doing due diligence on the organization to be acquired. This includes a very long, hard examination of the people, their values, their organizational cultures, their ways of working, and more, and it has proven to be very successful.

We had a client who was responsible for the merging of six very different organizations in a high-tech business all at once. He described them as having been "kluged together," and they did not want to be together. He had had two previous attempts to bring the leadership of the six organizations together in team-building off-sites, and both failed. These organizations were each performing a significant function in national security, so he had to get them willingly to work together. We applied our VBP processes, including some specific techniques to pull together both people and their different areas of business. By the end of the first three-day workshop, the participants had begun to talk about "we," "us," and "ours." By the end of the second workshop, they had completely *reorganized themselves* from six "stovepipes" into four new functionally based organizations. The critical factor here is that it was the participants who accomplished this. We got them to focus on the future, which took them out of their day-to-day differences and disagreements. It was an example of applying Albert Einstein's maxim *"We can't solve problems by using the same kind of thinking we used when we created them."* By thinking about the future, they developed a truly shared Vision, Mission and Values.

They identified Top-Level Goals, and then they asked themselves, "How can we achieve these?" Their best solution was by reorganizing. We returned to the organization almost two years later to help with an update to their strategic plan. It required very little in the way of change—just a few tweaks to one goal. Their original vision remained unchanged. However, the good news was that everything was working beautifully within their new organization and the members of the entire leadership team had become good friends as well as good colleagues.

Changing Mind-Sets

Changing cultures means changing mind-sets on a large scale. As individuals, our mind-sets are formed from very early childhood by representatives of the culture into which we are born—parents, teachers, friends—all of whom want to influence us to be good citizens of society as they view it. The society in which we live—in this context, not the national culture (although that does have some influence) but the fairly small area in which we grow up—results from that area's history, tradition, culture, religion, environment, norms, values, beliefs, and expectations for the future. For example, most countries in the West have neighborhoods of Caucasians, Blacks, Hispanics, and Asians. The people in each of those neighborhoods probably have some of the values and mores of the country in which they live, but also have the values, beliefs, religions, myths, and mores of their forebears. The children in each of those neighborhoods develop quite different mind-sets about many things. These mind-sets may not be as different from those of the indigenous national population as those of their immigrant parents; they are probably far more westernized. Even so, they still have different cultures, values, beliefs, religions, and views about marriage, gender roles, and so on.

Yet people do change their minds—through schooling, peer pressure, aging and maturing—but it usually happens in an evolutionary fashion. When we are children, the earth appears flat; that's all we see. Then we learn in school that the earth is round (although we still wonder why people in the Southern Hemisphere don't fall off). Then we fly in an airplane and see that the horizon is curved, and we look at pictures from space that show that the earth really is round (or rather, an oblate spheroid). That finally convinces us. However, while that logical, rational approach works when we consider "something out there," it has little impact on us personally. A purely rational approach does not suffice when we consider the future of an organization, which means people as much as it means product. To convince people to change, we also have to include a means to tap into and protect (as much as we are able) their emotions. This includes working with their values and ensuring that the organization reflects those values. If there is a mismatch between personal and organizational values, there will be friction.

Changing the mind-sets of a large group of people, and changing them significantly, means changing paradigms. These are the stories we tell ourselves that enable us to make sense of the world in which we live and in which we want to continue to live. Good stories include emotion, not just facts. The cultural approach to changing organizations therefore requires both leaders with vision, who can connect with their people, and good stories about why we need to change, including what we want to be and do in the future and how we plan to do it.

In his book *The Masks of War,* Carl Builder describes the substantial opposition to Trident submarine modernization in the UK. A sea-based nuclear weapons system, Trident was acquired by the UK government in the early 1980s as a replacement for the Polaris missile system, which the UK had possessed since the 1960s.[15] That opposition prompted the Ministry of Defense (MOD) to issue a white paper that included

---

15 Carl Builder, *The Masks of War: American Military Styles in Strategy and Analysis,*
    JHU Press, Baltimore, 1989.

many logical, rational arguments about strategic objectives, threats, and the like. They were good arguments, but few people found them compelling. Almost as an afterthought, the white paper mentioned that if Polaris subs were not modernized, the MOD would be unable to attract and retain the best people for its strategic nuclear forces. That somewhat emotional argument proved especially effective, but it hadn't been recognized by most senior officers or politicians.

Conventional wisdom tells us that most people don't like to change. That may have been truer before the days of widespread travel and communication, when people were more isolated and insular, but it is no longer always the case. From our values model described in Appendix 1, more than a third of the population in most Western countries (even more in the United States and Australia) is happy to change in certain ways—indeed, they create or embrace change, even for its own sake. More than a third of the population will change if they see that it is in their own best interests to do so, and less than a third actively resists change. A recent survey by Raconteur.net, a company in the UK that specializes in trends and reports for industry, showed that 57 percent of senior executives admitted that the pace of change was taking them by surprise, and 42 percent were concerned about their company's future relevance in the light of change. So clearly, there is a belief that people are not sufficiently open to change.

Thus, if we believe that we need to change the culture of an organization, *we must find the right stories to tell current and future employees.* We must enlist the support of those who welcome change; we need to show those who might consider changing why it is in their best interests to do so; and we need to bring along the rest by whatever persuasion we can muster, or else tell them to leave. However, before we go so far as dismissing them, we need to listen to their arguments for resisting change, because they are often the people who alert us to the advantages in the current situation that we do not want to lose—in other words, not "throwing the baby out with the bathwater."

Using Our VBP Process for Changing Cultures

Why change? In essence, you, the leader, believe and assert that the future will look significantly different from the past and even the present. While your organization may continue to do some similar things, it will do them in different ways. (This is the most obvious application of technology.) But new technologies and approaches may allow us to do many more new things than the old organization even dreamed of. So the emphasis on vision is important in changing culture. In developing this new vision, you must think futuristically and creatively before considering constraints, such as budgets, policies, and procedures. You must also think systemically, seeing the new organization as a total system and examining its roles and missions from that broad perspective.

Our VBP process lends itself beautifully to the process of changing cultures. While you could determine the new vision on your own, a vision developed by an entire leadership team (usually immediate subordinates who command sub-organizations or component divisions, and perhaps their immediate subordinates), plus other key stakeholders, commands far more buy-in and commitment. As we've said earlier, we suggest including a few young mavericks, as they are more likely to think more unconventionally than the older leadership. Only by creating this broad, shared perspective can the leadership of the various sub-organizations or component divisions see the benefits that the new vision and plan would bring to themselves and to their own organizations, even if they must reorganize to realize them. This takes courageous leaders who can not only lay out their ideas but also commit themselves to considering the ideas that emerge from the group.

In some situations, you may already have a vision and believe strongly in it, and must develop a plan to achieve it. Under those circumstances, you should make that vision as open and "unfinished" as possible so all stakeholders can interpret it in ways that make sense for their own parts of the organization. The emphasis, in this case, belongs on the ways in which various parts of the organization can contribute to the overall vision and plan.

It is worth noting that the Vision and Strategic Plan come first. Then the culture and organization is changed to facilitate the implementation of the plan. We have been amazed at how often we have seen the leadership of an organization try to "put the cart before the horse." The ideal way to accomplish this is during the VBP process. We need to start with the story of why the organization needs to change. What is happening in the external environment that necessitates change? What will happen if the organization doesn't change? We use all this as part of the Expansionary and Exploratory Phase in the VBP process. Having then developed the Vision, Mission, and Values, we then ask each participant how their part of the organization can contribute to making the Vision a reality. What can it contribute? What can it do? What can it develop? From the answers to those questions the Top-Level Goals and any eventual restructuring of the organization emerge. The restructuring and cultural changes are finalized after the participants have gone through the rest of the process. That is how it happened in the example given earlier in this Chapter of the high-tech organization with six divisions that were kluged together.

Figure 12-1: Strategic Planning Process

Figure 12-1 shows a different perspective on our VBP workshop process that we have found especially useful for changing cultures. At the top of the diagram are the future scenarios that are creating the need for change. We then gain consensus and commitment to the Vision, Mission, Values, Top-Level Goals, Strategies, Action, and Implementation Plans, and then we work out the implications for the cultural and organizational change.

Blocks to Change and How to Overcome Them

Some of the main blocks to change are the middle managers. These are frequently people who have been in the organization for some time, they (think) they know how it works, they don't like change, and they are sure that whatever changes are made will mean more work for them. This may seem rather cynical, but we have seen it and heard about it many times.

The first thing to do is to ensure that everyone in the organization knows what is in it for them. It may be the anticipation of increased pay or job opportunities. It may mean just getting them to understand that the changes will produce real benefit for the organization, which will eventually be passed on to them in some form. One of the techniques we often recommend is that you and your leadership team speak directly to the people on the shop floor, or at the pointy end of the spear. You explain that you want everyone to contribute to the new Vision, and if they have ideas about how they can do that, and you adopt them, you will give them an incentive bonus or prize. This not only results in some good ideas, but it puts pressure on the hesitant middle managers.

In summary, the three key ideas for changing cultures are:

1. Develop a new story that makes sense to most of the people involved. In organizational terms, this is usually the vision of what the organization should be, plus a description of what it wants to do, why it wants to do it, and how it wants to do it. Then communicate that story in ways that resonate with people—using elements of visual, auditory, and kinesthetic communication.

2. Identify and communicate "what's in it for them" to the people who are reluctant to change. Usually this is done best by involving the entire leadership of the organization to get buy-in and commitment.

3. Ensure that the values of the organization are aligned as closely as possible with those of its workforce.

One final comment about the VBP process: All members of the leadership who have participated in the workshops have the materials, worksheets, tools, and visual aids from them. We recommend that all the leaders go back to their organizations and take their subordinates through a similar, although shorter, process. The focus at this level should be "How can we, as a team, contribute to the overall Vision, Mission and Strategic Plan?" This approach to cascading the results down through the organization can be very powerful.

In some cases, where it is difficult for individuals in leadership or management to handle the change, yet it is critical, there are executive coaches who can be brought in to help.

Key Points from this Chapter

■ Increasingly fast-paced change in the external world is creating the need for organizational change.

■ Even when the leadership of an organization realizes that, they often experience significant resistance from the rest of their organization, especially middle management or mid-ranking officers.

■ You, the leadership, need to be very clear about the reasons for change—both logical (head) and emotional (heart)—and to communicate both effectively.

■ VBP produces:

• A strategy that is developed from both a logical/rational perspective (head) and a creative/emotional one (heart).

- Much greater buy-in and genuine commitment to the vision and strategic plan, resulting in a much smoother, faster, and more effective implementation.

CHAPTER 13

Now What?

Next Steps

Now that you have your VB Plan in hand, right down to the level of the Action and Implementation Plans, and you have the commitment from your leadership team, much of management, and a few mavericks, what happens next? This chapter describes everything from what you and your strategic planning team do, starting the day after the Phase 2 workshop, to how to update the plan on a regular basis, make major changes as necessary, and keep the Vision and plan going through a change in leadership.

The Implementation Plan describes how you will implement the VBP. We discussed the benefits of establishing a Strategic Planning Group, if you don't already have one, in order to keep the implementation on track. Remember, these people are not the designers and developers of the plan, they are a support function reporting directly to the CEO, and they need the support of the CEO to be able to hold people accountable for their parts of the VBP.

We have placed a lot of emphasis on the need to communicate the plan to all stakeholders, which is critical. All the participants in the VBP process should ensure they communicate it in detail to their subordinates, asking them how they can contribute to the new Vision.

Maintaining the Plan

Generally, we have found that a VBP developed this way will last at least two years without change and, as an example above, 14 years, although that is unusual. However, you must not assume that to be the case. You need to be vigilant. One of the things that needs to be done is to keep track of your external environment, not just your sales, but the STEEP issues in your external environment. This can be one of the roles of your Strategic Planning Group (SPG). Or you can find an organization that does "environmental tracking" and have their reports and newsletters evaluated by the SPG.

One of the best ways to do this is to have the key parts of the WarRoom on display—in a corridor or around a room—as recommended earlier. Members of the SPG can take their tracking data and walk around the WarRoom asking themselves if anything they are reading/seeing might affect any aspect of the plan. If it does, then they bring it to the attention of the appropriate manager. If it's a fairly insignificant change, then the manager deals with it himself, or brings in a small team to discuss it. If it's a major development that could impact the whole organization, then you, as leader, need to bring a team together to deal with it and alter the plan accordingly.

Approximately every 18 to 24 months, or at a change in leadership, it's worth going through a "sustaining the vision" session. This is generally a two-day workshop with the leadership (and, if necessary, including the new leader) where all of you go through:

- An assessment of where the organization is with respect to the Vision, Mission and Top-Level Goals.
  - This can be accomplished using the Development Curve method described in Chapter 9.
  - If your organization is not as far along in the achievement of a goal as it had anticipated, then take a look at the Objectives for the goal and go through the same Development Curve exercise with each Objective.

- Where there is below-par performance ask why? What's inhibiting the progress? Find the reasons and ask what the appropriate manager can do to overcome the blocks. If the problem is difficult to solve, then perhaps the time frame for the achievement of the Objective and goal needs to be extended.
- An assessment of whether the organization needs more Top-Level Goals, or any Objectives for the goals.
- An evaluation of any unexpected problems and potential solutions
- An evaluation of the entire organization in terms of how the participants are thinking about it *and feeling about it.*

Finally, there needs to be a commitment to address and resolve whatever new issues have come up.

If many things are changing in the external operating environment, or if some major decision is made for an acquisition or merger, for instance, then you should go through the complete VBP process again. When in doubt, go back to the WarRoom. Stare at it, walk through it, and ask yourself "What else?" and "What's missing?"

Above everything else, think strategically and encourage your leadership and management teams to think strategically. It seems to be a dying art, yet it is absolutely crucial for any organization that is serious about success. And get employees at all levels to think about how they might contribute to the Vision.

It's Up to You...

We hope we have been able to convince you of the value of vision-based planning for all organizations, but especially complex ones, and acquisition and mergers, as well as for the understanding and implementation of complex ideas or concepts.

We have emphasized that VBP is a leadership function, which cannot be delegated below the very top levels if it is to be successful. Leaders must own the process for their organization and participate personally to achieve a successful outcome. When a team is built, consensus is reached, and the leadership has personal ownership of the results, it fosters genuine passion—a critical requirement for success—in implementation of the new ideas and plans.

We have provided a step-by-step guide any leader can use. It may take a little time to develop the skills to work through the steps quickly and effectively, but it's worth it. Once the process has been mastered, it can be applied again—to the whole organization or just a part. Success is a choice founded on an ardent desire to achieve a Vision and the capability to attain it by getting the rest of the organization to not only buy into it but to become caught up in it.

To paraphrase our rhyme from the introduction:

> 'Tis the set of **your** sails and not the gales
> That determine the way you go

As we mentioned at the beginning of the book, we find VBP to be a rewarding and fun activity. It stretches us, causes us to think, and keeps our minds active and alive. We hope that it will do the same for you. We wish you the very best of luck and hope that this book will have made life easier for you. As they say in the Navy, we wish you "fair winds and following seas."

Key Points from this Chapter

- VBP is an ongoing process from the moment you return from the Phase 2 workshop.
- It includes routine updates as minor changes occur.
- It helps you deal with times of great internal and external change.
- It describes how you can build on all the good work you have accomplished in this first major VBP Process.
- And what you can do when changes and even unanticipated events occur.
- Remember, planning should be rewarding and fun.

Glossary of Key Terms

The problem with words is – they have meanings.

Complex Organization: Organizations that have many people, processes, rules, strategies, and basic units.

Compromise: To make a deal between different parties where each party gives up part of their demand. In arguments, compromise is a concept of finding agreement through communication, through a mutual acceptance of terms—often involving variations from an original goal or desire.

Consensus: General agreement or unanimity of group opinion; judgment arrived at by all or most concerned; group solidarity in sentiment and belief.

Conceptual versus Functional Planning: Plans can be either functional or conceptual. Conceptual planning, which may be either short or long range in application and effect, is principally concerned with the organization's future relationship with its external world. Based less on information generated internally to the organization than on external data sources, conceptual planning is directed toward identifying the organization's long-range goals and the establishment of broad policies, which set its future character and direction. Due to inherent uncertainties, conceptual planning most often deals with problems that are unstructured and irregular. Decisions in a conceptual planning process are often based on imprecise and incomplete data, and therefore, require an intuitive and creative approach.

Functional planning deals more with immediate organizational objectives, employing clearly defined, internally developed methods prescribed by top management to move the organization in a direction toward the achievement of goals. It is integral with the organization's formal resource allocation and investment process, normally proceeds in accordance with structured procedures and regular timetables, uses relatively accurate and reliable data, and is more routinely administrative in character.

Although, in theory, conceptual and functional planning can be thus distinguished, in practice the actual distinction may be less clear. Both involve generally similar procedures, but while conceptual planning usually describes preferred outcomes for the organization as a whole, functional planning addresses specific programs tailored to result in more precisely defined outcomes. Ideally, however, the functional goals will be congruent with and mutually support progress toward the broader goals developed through the conceptual planning process at the top of the organization.

Culture: There are many definitions of culture. For our purposes, the two provided here are the most useful:

1. "Culture: learned and shared human patterns or models for living day to-day living patterns. These patterns and models pervade all aspects of human social interaction. Culture is mankind's primary adaptive mechanism."[16]

2. "Culture is the collective programming of the mind, which distinguishes the members of one category of people from another."[17]

Dilemma: A dilemma is a decision that the organization must make that has only a range of less-than-satisfactory outcomes.

Forecasting: Forecasting is assessment of the future with some degree of confidence, by either quantitative or qualitative methods. It is useful in building the foundation for the understanding of the competitive environment—in a sense, "market analysis"—for a strategic planning effort, especially for complex organizations.

---

16 Damen, L. (1987). *Culture Learning: The Fifth Dimension on the Language Classroom.* Reading, MA: Addison-Wesley, p 367

17 Hofstede, G. (1984). National Cultures and Corporate Cultures. In L.A. Samovar & R.E. Porter (Eds.), *Communication Between Cultures.* Belmont, CA: Wadsworth.

Before performing costly strategic forecasts in support of long-range, as well as short-range, planning efforts, it is useful to understand the reasons why you might want to forecast in the first place. For example, an organization might want to perform environmental or strategic forecasting as a broadening exercise for the participants. It might even be done for the enlightenment and entertainment (a`la Herman Kahn – an early and larger-than-life futurist) of top management. Or it could be done to enhance the quality of strategic planning and decision-making. Whatever the reason, it should always be clearly understood that long-range planning and strategic forecasting efforts are generally expensive, both in terms of dollars, equipment, and the time of highly talented people. For success, the organization should understand the reasons for doing it, know what its focus should be, and it should emphasize doing it well. If not, at worst it could lead to planning disasters; at best, it will waste valuable, scarce resources.

In the Positive: When referring to goals and objectives, statements should be "in the positive"—something beneficial and positive to be accomplished, rather than an outcome to be avoided (a negative statement).

Long-Range Planning: One key term in the context of this book is long-range planning. Long-range planning has been defined as "the process through which top managers identify their long-term objectives and establish broad policies and strategies to guide the acquisition, allocation, and use of resources to achieve those objectives. By comparison, with the functional planning done for an organization's annual programming and budgeting process, long-range planning is inherently less structured, more intuitive, and almost always concerned with factors beyond the organization's control. The result is a statement of ends and means."[18] Distinguishing between forecasts and plans is important. While plans describe the organization's view of what is sup-

---

18 Riggle, Gordon G. (1980). Looking to the Long Run. United States Naval Institute Proceedings, September 1980, p 60

posed to happen in the future, or at least what it would prefer to have happen, forecasts establish what might occur in the future, under a range of specified conditions or assumptions. Thus, forecasting is a means to an end—the end being the reduction of uncertainties in the future in order to minimize the impact of these uncertainties on decisions being made in the present, according to planning guidelines and goals.

In the common usage of organizational planners, short-term planning generally concerns the current fiscal or budget year, and the early (usually no more than the first two) years of any longer range plan. Mid-range plans usually encompass the period from beyond two years to as far out as eight years. Extended planning covers the period from the end of the mid-range plans to up to 10 years beyond. Beyond long-range planning is a form of conceptual planning.

Maverick: A young, high-energy person in an organization, who is a constant fountain of new and unusual ideas, usually about doing things differently. Often, they are regarded as irritants, to whom the leadership does not listen.

Measure: A measure generally has an element of human judgment; it is generally about the *what* that is to be measured.

Metric: A metric is an indicator or value that can be observed singly or collectively; for example, time, length of turn, speed, distance, and other countable events. Metrics are directly measurable and generally form the answers related to the *how* and *how well* of outcome achievement or system performance.

Mission: A mission (or purpose) is what the organization does or is for; it is generally written using action verbs.

Projection: Projection is the extension into the future of past historical trends, by some systematic method.

Prophecy: Prophecy is prediction by divine inspiration.

Prediction: Prediction is statement of fact before the event.

Stakeholder: Stakeholders are people within and outside your organization who have a stake in your future success. You need to be aware of all of them and how to relate to them. We suggest that some of the key external ones participate in your planning process, along with your leadership. Note that there are such persons as *negative stakeholders*. These fall into two categories—those who criticize and complain about you and your organization and those who stand to benefit from your failure to succeed. It can sometimes be useful to have some of the former participate in the expansionary/exploratory sessions of your workshops, as they can provide useful insight

Strategic Plan: A strategic plan is the outcome of a strategic planning effort of an organization or group. It generally includes a statement of the organization's or group's vision, mission or purpose, values, top-level goals, and strategies to execute them. A good strategic plan is actionable and represents a consensus of the organization or group that prepared it.

Strategic Planning: Strategic planning, in the formal sense, "...is inextricably interwoven into the entire fabric of management; it is not something separate and distinct from the process of management."[19] George Steiner, in his book *Strategic Planning*, characterizes strategic planning, which he considers synonymous with long-range or corporate planning, with futurity, process, philosophy, and structure.[20] More specifically, strategic planning looks at the "futurity of current decisions, at the chain of cause-and-effect consequences over time of an actual or intended decision that a manager is going to make [and] also the alternative courses of action that are open in the future."[21] Steiner adds that "the essence of formal strategic planning is the systematic identification of opportunities and threats that lie in the future, which in combination with other relevant data, provide a basis for [an organization's] making better current decisions to exploit the opportunities and avoid the threats."[22]

---

19 Steiner, George A. (1979). *Strategic Planning: What Every Manager Must Know.* New York: The Free Press, p. 3
20 See ibid., pp. 13-15
21 Ibid., p. 13
22 Ibid., pp.13-14

Strategic planning is also a process, beginning with the setting of organizational aims, defining strategies to achieve them, and developing detailed plans to ensure strategies are implemented. Strategic planning can provide an organization with a philosophy—an attitude, a thought process, a way of life——"a determination to plan constantly and systematically as an integral part of management; an intellectual exercise [where] managers and staff in an organization must believe strategic planning is worth doing as well as they can."[23]

Finally, strategic planning provides structure that links "strategic plans, medium-range programs, and short-range budgets and operating plans; through the linkages, top management strategies are translated into current decisions." To summarize, strategic planning is the systematic and more or less formalized effort of an organization to establish basic purposes, objectives, policies and strategies, and to develop detailed plans to implement policies and strategies to achieve objectives and basic organizational purposes.

Unmentionables: These are ideas or thoughts that, if brought up in a meeting of the organization's leadership, would cause the person expressing the idea or thought to be admonished and expelled immediately from the meeting (or worse). The speaking aloud of unmentionables generally evokes strong responses and feelings within the organization's leadership group. The value of unmentionables is that they often expose serious, yet unstated problems within the organization, and therefore must be dealt with as new visions, values, and strategic plans are developed.

Values: Values are deeply held beliefs that have a strong emotional component. To be meaningful, they must be lived.

Vision: A vision is what an organization will become, or where it is going. It is generally written using existential verbs.

Vision-Based Planning (VBP): Our Vision-Based Planning process is a way of enabling complex organizations to realize their strategic

---

23 Ibid., p. 14

vision, through achievement of their strategic goals, despite a future filled with change and uncertainty.

- Features of a robust, vision-based strategic planning process include:

- Helping the organization to form a new, robust strategic vision, ideally based on a reframed view of the organization, shared by all or most of its key stakeholders

- Helping the organization develop and implement the appropriate means for working toward and realizing the vision, by defining clear top-level goals and strategies

- Preparing the top leadership of the organization to understand, anticipate, and deal with change, however discontinuous or unanticipated—ideally, to understand and exploit change.

- Providing and developing information of value to the top leadership, allowing minimization of unanticipated events affecting the future of the organization.

- Producing buy-in and consensus throughout the organization.

WarRoom: The WarRoom, as created and used by us in our VBP work, is an approach to the development, transcription, and systematic display of all materials and results prepared by the team, from the beginning of the expansion phase to the completion of the synthesis stage, which allows each participant to track the development of ideas and results, and to see their results displayed in a clear and an immediately actionable format. Each WarRoom is unique to the team and the solutions sought. The WarRoom is also a valuable tool to help participants educate others who did not participate in the VBP process to understand how such key elements of the results such as the vision, values, top-level goals, and stakeholder plans were developed.

Workshop: An intensive, interactive session with an organization's top leadership, along with selected other participants, designed to achieve practical and actionable results.

Social Values Models

This Appendix is derived from previous work by Applied Futures. For the values data we want to thank our colleagues and friends Les Higgins and Pat Dade from Cultural Dynamics Strategy & Marketing in the UK. They have taken Applied Futures' original social values models and have expanded and updated them considerably. They have also applied them to many more countries, including India, China, Southeast Asia, Australia, and Latin America.

The Value of Values

Values underpin every aspect of society, including its culture, politics, economy, industry, attitudes, consumption, and even the development of technology. Thus, values provide a basis by which to understand the context within which people live and operate in a society. They provide us with a deep understanding of people—as employees, consumers, and other stakeholders—and enable us to communicate with them much more effectively than through any other means.[24]

Values are emotional constructs that underpin attitudes and behavior (see Figure A1-1 below). They are closely related to beliefs, which are convictions that are held to be true by individuals or groups, and they are also related to psychological needs. They are longer term—people generally have them for anything from 10 years to a lifetime, and they change slowly. They underpin attitudes that can be held for 2 to 10

---

24 Chris Rose, *Op Cit*

years, while behavior is short term, generally less than two years duration. Beliefs are long-held perceptions that have generally been inculcated from birth by family, teachers, and leaders of the society, although they can and do change slowly over time. In some cases, they may change quickly, generally through some extreme (good or bad) event. Motivations are the factors that compel a person or group to act, and they are functions of values, beliefs, and needs. Understanding motivations helps us understand *why* people do what they do. Behavior tells us *what* people are doing. If we understand the *why*, we have a greater chance to anticipate what people are likely to do next.

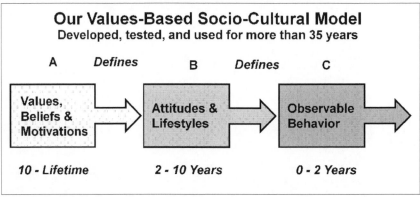

Figure A1-1 Values Underpin Behavior

We have used our values models very successfully for multinational commercial organizations, government institutions, and even for forecasting political changes in various countries for more than 35 years. Our values model is based on Maslow's Hierarchy of Needs,[25] and augmented by the work of Shalom Schwartz,[26] Geert Hofstede,[27] Ron Inglehart,[28] and others.

---

25 Maslow, Abraham, *Motivation and Personality,* Harper Row, NY 1954, 1987, pp15-45.

26 Schwartz, Shalom; Melech, Gila; Lehmann, Arielle; Burgess, Steven; Harris, Mari; Owens, Vicki, *"Extending the Cross-Cultural Validity of the Theory of Basic Human Values with a Different Method of Measurement,"* Journal of Cross-Cultural Psychology. 2001 Sep Vol 32(5).

27 Hofstede, Geert, *Cultures and Organizations,* McGraw-Hill International (UK) 1991.

28 Ronald Inglehart, *Modernization and Postmodernization,* Princeton University Press, Princeton, NJ, 1997.

The objective of our values analysis is to sort any population into subgroups based on their values, beliefs, and motivations. Since values underpin motivations, we focus on the core set of values that might compel or influence a group that holds a particular set of values. We can segment the population according to the different values particular subgroups hold. Using values for this purpose is quite different and provides a much greater depth of analysis than psychographics.

In the West, we use the 21 Schwartz Values Portraits questions, plus 25 that we have developed and tested over the last 35 years. Until recently, for non-Western countries, we have used only the value sets and questions developed by Schwartz, as those have been tested and validated in 74 countries, but we have now added further questions to surveys for other parts of the world. In addition, we add questions on what we call attributes. Our instrument for determining cultural values used to be a face-to-face survey of the population of interest. Although we frequently use online surveys today, we realize we are not getting completely representative samples that way. However, since we are generally interested in younger and better educated populations that is not a problem. If we need older populations who have less access to the internet, we can return to face-to-face interviews. Along with the values questions, we have questions on decision-making, media usage, ownership/usage of various items, influence/advice, attitudes and behavior. We then cross-tabulate the values and the typologies we develop with the rest of the questions to provide a very rich picture of the population.

We perform statistical analyses on the results to arrange the responses in a two-dimensional map (see Figure A1-2 that uses the 21 Schwartz portrait values). When we use the map to display the values of an entire population, the results are neutral. When we put the values of a subgroup onto the map, then we can identify outlier values—what we call "hot" and "cold" buttons—that distinguish each of the subgroups. We use these values as a basis for understanding them and crafting the appropriate messages for the subgroup. Let us look at these subgroups at both micro and macro levels.

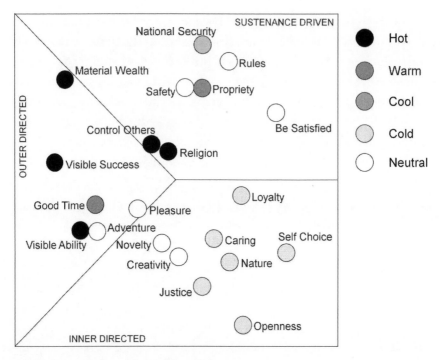

Figure A1-2: Values Map of One Subgroup

Micro-Level of Values Subgroups

This is the level of individuals and small groups. In general terms, we have identified three broad Value Groups, each of which has a number of subsets. But for our purposes, the descriptions of the three broad groups is enough.

Inner Directed Group

This group made up approximately 50 percent of the U.S. population and 41 percent of the UK in 2012.

The Inner Directed Group is so named because its members derive their sense of personal direction, their personal rewards, and their criteria for success from within themselves. The standards by which Inner Directeds measure themselves and the world tend not to be the materialistic standards of wealth, social class, income, status, or possession,

STRATEGY WITH PASSION

but rather they are standards involving such things as integrity, honesty, quality, and appropriateness to the situation. Inner Directeds are the most psychologically mature of the groups, yet they are still seeking greater maturity. Although most are not anti-materialistic, they consider people rather than things to be of paramount importance, so they tend to see people in ways that have far greater human significance than the social role of membership in a class or the economic role of producer/consumer.

Their introspection is a characteristic that makes these people very easy to misunderstand, and it is important not to confuse inner directedness with introversion or self-centeredness. What they do is to try to maximize their own, individual, potential, but they generally seek to do that in a way that is not exploitive of others.

Inner Directed people are difficult to observe because the thing that distinguishes them from the rest of the population is their *motivation* rather than their *behavior*, and as a result of this the media has real difficulty in presenting inner directedness. Inner Directeds tend to be self-confident, and although they are by no means anti-social, they do not feel obliged to conform to stereotyped social norms.

It seems likely that it is the combination of their self-confidence and their inner sense of what is important in their lives that gives the Inner Directed group its significant role as trendsetters in society. During the past 35 years, almost every major trend in Western society has been started by this group, although the trends have then been picked up and driven, as fashion, by Outer Directeds (see below). In proportion to its size, the Inner Directed group has a greater influence in almost every area.

Outer Directed Group

In contrast to Inner Directed people, Outer Directed people made up approximately 32 percent of the U.S. population and 28 percent of the UK in 2012. Unlike Inner Directeds, Outer Directeds rely heavily on external indicators of their own self-worth. To put it another way, an

Outer Directed person's concept of himself depends on his being able to achieve more than his peers.

Outer Directed needs are centered on esteem. Therefore, at work the Outer Directed person is conscious of, and seeks actively to acquire, status and the symbols related to it. Such people are very much at home in structured, hierarchical organizations in which they can establish their position clearly and then display their position and measure their progress relative to others. In identifying themselves with a peer group in this way, Outer Directeds automatically judge themselves to be up to the group's level, and they generally use the group as the source of the standards by which they judge their world. The people in this group are of vital social importance; they are the dynamo, the energy source in our society. They are the ones who feel the need to compete, who need to prove themselves against the opposition, who have the drive to win at virtually any cost.

Sustenance Driven Group

Everywhere we look in Western industrial society, the two groups that we have just considered have been growing at the expense of a third group, which we call the Sustenance Drivens. This pattern has been a consistent trend for some time, although the recent recession has had some impact here, and some countries have seen what we believe to be a short-term increase in this group. However, because of its generally declining size (approximately 18 percent of the U.S. population and 31 percent of the UK in 2012), we consider the direct impact of the Sustenance Driven group on the long-term future of Western countries to be relatively small. However, they are influential at the moment, and to neglect them would be to miss the essential role by which they will influence the future. Indeed, if the industrialized countries experience significant immigration from the developing world, this group will probably increase in size.

Sustenance Driven needs are deficiency needs, and the distinguishing characteristic of Sustenance Driven people is a desire to "hold what you've got." This orientation tends to make them form homogeneous groups with well-defined characteristics and relatively impermeable boundaries. The typical picture this idea brings to mind is the tightly knit, clannish, working-class or rural community. A little reflection will indicate that these characteristics also describe a good many company directors of the "old school," a lot of the traditional professions, not to say a good many politicians. In fact, we find that the Sustenance Driven groups include a substantial number of people from all these conventional classifications, and the thing that they have in common is that they resist change. Not only do they hold on to their possessions but to their institutions as well.

Within each of these broad groups, we may have up to four subgroups, depending on the particular country/culture and the purpose for which we are using them. We generally use these broad groupings for strategic planning, marketing planning, and R&D planning, while we use the 12 subgroups for advertising and more targeted messages.

If we have a large enough sample (approximately 5,000 people for most countries) to allow us to "slice and dice" the survey results into small segments, we can determine the values of specific small samples—people who own Ford cars versus Porsches, by age, region, and media habits, for instance. Or we can identify the values of people who prefer complementary medicine to allopathic medical approaches by age and education levels, for instance. We have had enormous success helping clients develop new products and brands, and new advertising and marketing strategies using values.

Macro Level Values Subgroups

We can look at the values held by different nations and evaluate the overall tendencies of a particular country based on its values. For cross-country comparison, the three broad groups—Inner Directed (ID), Outer Directed (OD), and Sustenance Driven (SD), derived from Maslow—are most useful (see Figure A1-3).

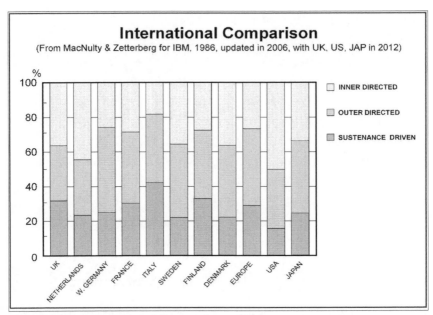

International Comparison

(From MacNulty & Zetterberg for IBM, 1986, updated in 2006, with UK, US, JAP in 2012)

%

INNER DIRECTED

OUTER DIRECTED

SUSTENANCE DRIVEN

UK NETHERLANDS W. GERMANY FRANCE ITALY SWEDEN FINLAND DENMARK EUROPE USA JAPAN

Figure A1-3: International Comparison of Values

The comments that follow are trivial—we could write a book on the cultural differences indicated in Figure A1-3—but we want to give you a taste. In this picture, we see that the United States is predominantly Inner Directed (50 percent), although it has large numbers of Outer Directed (32 percent). These numbers have reversed over the last decade, despite the recession. It has the smallest number of Sustenance Driven people in the West (18 percent). This combination of values is what gives the United States its outgoing, entrepreneurial characteristics, the desire to succeed, and predominantly capitalist economic system. We place significant emphasis on individualism, and we expect people to be able to make decisions for themselves. We have difficulty understanding people in cultures where the collective is much stronger, such as the Middle East, for instance, which is predominantly Sustenance Driven. In the UK, which has recently seen a resurgence of Sustenance values, and some European countries, we see a combination of large Inner Directed and Sustenance Driven groups, which tends to create a greater interest in social welfare and socialist systems.

What Can We Do with the Data?

Communications

One major area for use of this values information is marketing, advertising, influence, and other communications. Messages that are directed toward values can resonate with people the way messsages related to behavior do not.

Generally, we have applied our advertising and strategic communications campaigns to promote certain behavior; and values can help significantly with those intentions, although we also need to understand and incorporate the context of the situation as well. However, there is an important element here: People are very reluctant (absent force) *to act in opposition to their values.* Consequently, understanding values allows us to craft advertising and strategic communications campaigns and even develop products and services that would not be failures because of inherent resistance.

Narratives

Narratives are stories that pull together aspects of an organization or concept into a context. When developing scenarios for planning and R&D, we put great emphasis on narratives as they help people understand what we are doing and why. If we are developing an understanding of cultures with which we, personally, are not familiar, we will bring in subject matter experts to help us develop descriptive narratives of the people, their ways of life, their cultures and more.

At the very least, knowing the values and the cross-tabulations with attitudinal and behavioral data from the survey, enables us to create narratives about the different target groups, including the media habits of those groups. Those narratives can provide us with an enormous amount of information about what media to use, the content, tone, speed, music, and types of people to be used in developing the message.

Even better narratives can be developed if we can combine all our survey data with the experience of these SMEs who can tell us about a foreign country, and turn them into stories for Guided Imagination. For instance, in a workshop on an international aid program, the participants were trying to identify what the local population might need and how the United States might help them. Working with Dr. Claire Metelits, who had lived in the country for some time, we created a narrative that included word pictures of the physical environment. We wanted the participants to use their imaginations, so we guided them across terrain that Claire knew well. She described a walk down a mountainside to a village, stopping for a while at a picnic spot that was a favorite of the locals. She described not only the food that was being cooked, but the pastimes in which the villagers were engaged, including the men dancing. As she described the walk, I asked questions about weather, the countryside, odors, animals, villagers, including children, and villages. By the end of this Guided Imagination narrative, the participants in the workshop had a completely new understanding of what the villagers were like and what their needs were likely to be.

Forecasting using Values

Values are long term, attitudes are medium term, and behavior is short term, as Figure A1-1 indicated. If all we have available is behavioral data, then the only forecasting method available to us is some form of extrapolation of that behavior. But behavior is very fickle and can be altered by external events of many kinds. If we want to forecast behavior—of a large population or small group—the most reliable way is to understand the underlying values and motivations, how they are changing, and then anticipate how those changes are likely to play out in behavior. Extrapolating values—especially using the values hierarchy, such as that of Abraham Maslow—is relatively easy. For instance, in the United States, we saw the Inner Directed population increase consistently over the 30-year period from the late '70s to today (according to data from SRI International, the International Research Institute on Social Change, Cultural Dynamics Strategy & Marketing, and others), while the Sustenance Driven population declined. The Outer Directed population, sandwiched between the other two groups, saw some decline at one time, but increased more recently. Similar patterns were observed for many European countries, although the changes were not quite so marked.

On the basis of understanding how values were changing, we were able to forecast many different behavior patterns. We anticipated the healthy eating trends and increasing interest in both preventive and alternative medicine for many of our client companies. We anticipated the increased interest in physical fitness and diets. We anticipated the trends in SUVs and other "combination" vehicles, despite increasing concerns about the environment, and, later, the increase in "green" vehicles.

We believe that the more people use values as a basis for understanding their organizations and their business, the more successful they will be.

Minimizing Unanticipated Consequences of Nth Order Effects

Why go to all this trouble?

Nth order effects are much more important than most people realize—that is where the idea of unanticipated consequences comes from—and why we generally work through them with the decision makers involved in the actions or strategic communication. Indeed, the most effective way to accomplish the development of the action or message is by having the experts from several disciplines and even organizations working together. Most people are aware of first-order effects—generally the ones they want to achieve—in other words, their intent. And they may be aware of some second-order effects, which they refer to as potential downsides or upsides. However, there can be more. In this chapter we will use an example of a real-life situation to describe how to think about Nth order effects, as this one has been well-documented.

We have found that a combination of techniques for analyzing Nth order effects that rely heavily on subjective judgment can work quite well.

The four key elements in identifying and understanding Nth order effects are:

1. Understand the total system or system of systems and the context(s) in which it is to be considered.

2. Understand all the people involved: all "four estates," educators, industrialists/financiers, activists/radicals…and more.

3. Understand the relationships between the people/groups and between them and the system.

4. Develop relevant "what-if? mini scenarios" of the people/groups and the systems.

We have a combination of techniques for analyzing Nth order effects that include Mind-Maps (Chapter 9) for understanding the total system, our values models (Appendix 1) for understanding people, and we also have a system of weighted matrices derived from decision impact analysis and cross-support analysis[29] for understanding the relationships. This was a technique designed to analyze the effects of making and implementing complex decisions that affect and are affected by a large number of factors. Although, at the time, computing power was limited, so modeling and simulation was not an option, there were benefits to be had by working through the impacts in person, and we still prefer to do it that way. Then we pull all those three elements together in "What If?" scenarios.

Tragic Example

We are providing a description of Darwin's Nightmare, *a documentary movie produced by Hubert Sauper. We are including this as a cautionary tale, as it is a tragic strategic planning failure, with unanticipated Nth order effects. And, at the end, we will provide a brief description of how we might have tackled it using our techniques.*

---

29 Christine A. Ralph (MacNulty) "The Beginnings of Cross-Support Analysis as Applied to the Fishing Industry" in Cetron and Ralph, *Industrial Applications of Technological Forecasting,* John Wiley & Sons, NY, 1971, pp274-289.

What began as well-intended idea resulted in a colossal failure to understand the strategic context in which they were working, perhaps through a failure of vision and lack of thorough strategic planning— where Nth order effects occurred, in a terrible succession of unfortunate outcomes.

The European Demand for Fish

Throughout the '60s, '70s, and into the '80s, the European fishing industry declined precipitously. Overfishing in the North Sea, the Northern Atlantic, and the Mediterranean had reduced the quantities of fish available, just at a time when consumers were starting to become more health conscious and wanted more fish. The European Fish Processing Industry had collapsed to two major fish processing plants: one in the UK (East Anglia) and one in the Netherlands. At the same time, the technology of fast freezing and chilling fish at sea opened new opportunities for processing and transporting fish from around the world to satisfy European demand.

Helping Tanzania

Tanzania lies at the Southern end of Lake Victoria, a relatively calm country surrounded by the more politically troubled countries of Rwanda, Burundi, and the Democratic Republic of the Congo to the west, and Zambia, Malawi, and Mozambique to the south. Mwanza, a city close to the Lake, is the third largest city in Tanzania, with reasonable road infrastructure and a small, fairly primitive airfield/airport.

Sometime in the '60s, a voracious fish—the Nile Perch—was introduced into the lake. No one knows exactly when or by whom, or whether it was done by accident or design. The fish ate everything in the lake and bred rapidly. Although it will eat its own offspring, the lake was full of these fish during the late 1990s and early 2000s. When the fish is filleted, it looks like, and has the texture and flavor of Sea Bass—a fish highly prized by European consumers.

So the European Union helped to establish a fish processing plant on Lake Victoria, close to Mwanza. The European Union officials (including the Italian president of the EU) held an official opening ceremony, at which they spoke about the economic benefits of the plant to the Tanzanians and the benefits of the fish for the Europeans. They believed they were doing a good thing providing monetary and development assistance for Tanzania. They were taken on a tour of the plant, and in the documentary, we see the high-tech interior of the plant. The locals, with the help of the Europeans began developing fish farming to keep the fish from eating their offspring and to keep an available supply.

However, there was one major part of the plant that was missing, which would have prevented it from being allowed to operate in Europe. It had no means for disposing of the fish heads, offal, and carcasses. In European plants, the good fish fillets and the other remains get divided onto two separate moving belts. One takes the good fillets to the packing plant, and the other takes the remains away to be turned into soup, pet food, or agricultural fertilizer. In the movie, we see the unwanted remains being dropped out of a chute into trucks or on the ground. Whatever fell on the ground was shoveled up and put back in the trucks. It was taken to a place nearby and was dumped on the ground. We saw it rotting and covered in maggots; we saw kids playing with it—and we saw local women and older kids picking it up, putting it out on drying racks, smoking it, and frying it, and eating it. Did the Europeans notice this? Or could they have predicted the effects this one missing element could have caused?

The rotting fish and the stench/smoke from all the smoking and frying turned the place into a real health hazard. We saw pictures of women and children suffering from respiratory problems and blindness. It became clear that, aside from the fish processing plant itself, there were no clean and sanitary places around—no water except the lake, no sanitation, and no housing of any kind.

Meanwhile, word of this new industry got around the lake, and young men came seeking work, leaving behind wives and families. Prostitution became another significant industry, with young women servicing both the workers at the plant and the pilots of the air trans-porters. This resulted in an increased number of men and prostitutes with HIV/AIDS. When the men returned home, they took the HIV/AIDS with them. Along with the prostitution came drugs, and the drugs became increasingly available to children.

In other words, the whole area—from the ecosystem in the lake to the lives of the majority of people living in the area—took a downward turn.

Transportation and Weapons

At this time, the neighboring countries of Rwanda, Burundi, and the Congo were experiencing uprisings and tribal conflict, for which they needed weapons.

We do not know whether the EU officials were aware that the Ilyushin Il-76 was a better airplane for transporting weapons than fish, or whether they turned a blind eye to it, since it offered a relatively cheap form of transportation. When asked what was in the airplanes on the return journeys to Mwanza, the Russian pilots said "nothing," although it became clear to Hubert Sauper, the producer and director of the documentary who photographed them that they were smuggling in large collections of weapons. Others talked about some grain and other commodities being imported from Europe. One interesting fact, however, was that the Dutch Fisheries Hub and Amsterdam Airport, Schiphol, were chosen instead of London Airport, Heathrow, and the East Anglian Fisheries Hub. The reason given was that security was too much of a problem and time-consuming at Heathrow.

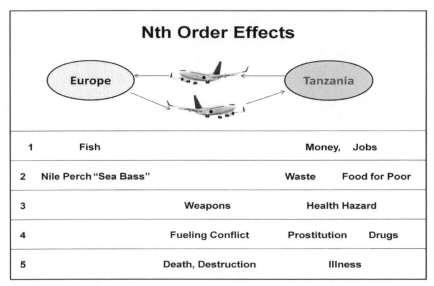

Figure A2-1: Nth Order Effects

When we analyzed the whole situation, we could see that there were five levels of effects. The first-order effects were good, then they got progressively worse, as seen in Figure A2-1.

Conclusions

The Europeans believed that they were doing some good in Tanzania by providing the fish processing plant that brought money and jobs to the area. And they were benefitting European consumers at the same time. Until this movie was made, they had no idea of the disaster they had caused in the area, and many still do not believe they had a hand in it.

They had no understanding of the strategic context, even for establishing a fish processing plant. They had even less understanding of the local socio-political environment that underpinned that part of the world. The only two groups that really benefitted were the European consumers and the weapons smugglers.

The moral of the tale is that the more we can understand of the strategic context in which we find ourselves, the better.

Our Analysis and Recommendations

Obviously, in hindsight, we can do a much better job of assessing Nth order effects than at the beginning of the processing plant development. But just taking the basic principles from our approach, we can apply them to the situation as the decision to build the fish processing plant was being made.

The first thing we would have done would have been to examine the operations associated with the fish processing plant, from the fish farming all the way to the shipment of fish to Schipol as a complete system. We could use a mind-map here, although, since this situation is relatively simple, a very rough flow diagram of the process together with a number of critical questions is enough—as in the diagram below. The diagram below gives the rough outline of some of the issues that should have been considered, and questions that could have been asked. Indeed, any competent systems analyst or systems engineer could have laid out the basic processes in much greater detail than this, and asked many more questions of the sort indicated in Figure A2-2 below. (It took the author about 15 minutes to think up and draw this diagram.)

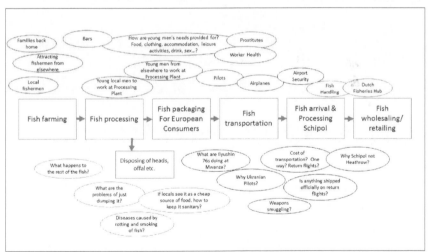

Figure A2-2 – Rough diagram of Fishing Operations, Issues and Questions

These issues and questions could have formed the basis for several mind-maps. From these and more issues and questions, we could have developed a list of causal and dependent variables from which to prepare several cross-support matrices—starting with one relating the whole fish processing business to the other variables, and then relating the variables to each other, as in the very brief example of the matrix below.

	Demand for fish	Fish Farming	Fish Processing	Supply skilled labor	Workers' needs	Worker health	Entertainment	Bars		
Demand for fish		H	H	-H	L	L				
Fish Farming	-M		H	-M						
Fish Processing	M	M		-M						
Supply skilled labor		M	M		M		M	M		
Workers' needs			L	M		M	H	H		
Worker health			H	M			-M	-M		
Entertainment					-M	-H		H		

Figure A2-3 – Simple matrix indicating causal relationships

Several people in our working group would have participated in completing this matrix, and we would have discussed each element.

So, for instance, we would have taken each row variable in turn (as causal) and asked how much does this variable affect each column variable? And we rate it on a scale of High (H), Medium (M), Low (L) and Zero (Blank) – positively or negatively (plus or minus) as appropriate. Thus the impact of Demand for Fish has a High impact on Fish Farming and Fish Processing, as it provides an impetus for both, but a –H (minus H) on Supply of Skilled Labor, as the increase of work at the Fish Farming and Processing facilities will reduce the pool of available skilled labor. We assign weights to the scores: H=8, M=4, L=2, Zero=1 (both positive and negative) so that later we can assess the priorities by adding the scores for the rows and/or columns, depending on what we are wanting to do with the scores. Frequently we need to have discussions within the group to get at the real issues that emerge from asking what the impacts are. Sometimes the answers can be quite complex, and if there appear to be several possibilities, then we may need to re-work the issues into more detailed sub-issues to make sure we are not canceling out effects by having too general an issue.

Then, we can use these matrices to ask "what if..?" type questions. Such as:

- What if we need more skilled labor in the processing plant than is available locally?
  - Where can we obtain it?
  - If the men have to travel long distances to get to the factory, so that they need to stay for some extended time, what happens to their families?
    - Can their families come with them?
      - If not, what provision do we need to make to provide food, accommodation, entertainment...for the men?
      - How frequently and for how long can they return home?
- What is the geo-political environment like in Mwanza and surrounding areas?
  - What are political and economic opportunities?
  - What are political and economic threats?
- What if these airplanes are not returning empty, as their pilots claim?
  - What might they carry that is beneficial to the country?
  - What might they carry that is not beneficial?
- What if all these opportunities have an impact similar to the gold-rush in the San Francisco area?
  - What if a new industry in bars and brothels opens?
  - What if the Russian pilots facilitate this new industry?
  - How can we keep the workers and their families healthy?
  - What if they attract undesirable people?

In more general terms, we often use a single matrix to display both causal and dependent variables and the relationships between them.

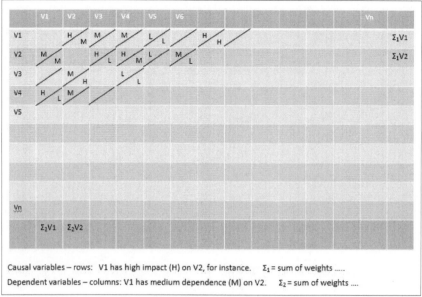

Figure A2-4 – More complex matrix showing both causal and dependent relationships

Once we have the matrices completed, we try to be as detailed as possible in identifying the "what ifs?" One good approach is to ask questions such as: "What would happen if Causal variable V1 increased significantly over the next 12 months? What would be its impacts on V2 to Vn?" Or what would happen if Causal variables V3, V4, V9, V10 all increased at the same time? The possibilities are endless.

Our social values model described in Appendix 1 can enrich these "what if?" questions, because we can use them to understand the motivations of the players. And then from them we then build scenarios of the short- medium- and longer-term developments that we anticipate, from the perspective of identifying opportunities and threats. Agent Based Modeling & Simulation (ABMS) can offer a method of actively modeling a system in such a way that the simulations are adaptable, repeatable, and deterministic, and it lends itself extremely well to these kinds of "what-if?" questions and scenarios.

If the EU had conducted even a simple form of this kind of analysis, it could have evaluated the importance of the issues and to focus on appropriate solutions, such as having proper disposal for the fish offal that could have included turning it into edible food for the locals. Or using aircraft from the EU to transport the fish to Europe, and return with products that would benefit the locals, rather than providing weapons to be used in neighboring conflicts.

Index

STRATEGY WITH PASSION

ABOUT THE AUTHORS

Christine A. R. MacNulty, FRSA

 Christine MacNulty has forty years of experience as a consultant in long-term strategic planning for concepts as well as organizations, futures/foresight, technology forecasting, technology assessment, and related areas, as well as socio-cultural change. Early in her career she began to use workshops to gain leadership commitment to their strategic plans. For the last 20 years, most of her consulting work has been conducted for the Department of Defense. She has provided consulting services for various Fortune Global 500 companies in the United States, the UK, and Western and Eastern Europe for client applications, including marketing, advertising, personnel and human resources, education, and training. MacNulty has also contributed methods and models for understanding social and cultural change, and at the request of several of her clients, she is now offering coaching in change and transformation, as well as strategic consultation.

She was elected a Fellow of the Royal Society of Arts, Manufactures and Commerce in 1988. She is the coauthor of two books: *Industrial Applications of Technology Forecasting* (Wiley) and *Strategy with Passion: A Leader's Guide to Exploiting the Future.* Her monograph "Truth, Perception & Consequences" was published by the Army War College (September 2007) and "Transformation: From the Outside In or the Inside Out" was also published by the Army War College (September 2008). Her paper: "Method for minimizing the negative consequences of nth order effects in strategic communication actions and inactions" was published in *NATO Defence Strategic Communications Journal,* Winter 2015. Her paper, "Perceptions, Values & Motivations in Cyberspace" appeared in the *IO Journal*, (3rd Quarter, 2009), and "The Value of Values" for IO, SC & Intel was published in the *IO Journal* (August 2010). She has been featured on the *Heartbeat of America* television program as the owner of an innovative small business. She was also the developer and co-host of the radio program "Strategy with Passion" that aired on VoiceAmerica.com Business Channel from May-December 2009.

Stephen R. Woodall, Ph.D.

Dr. Stephen R. Woodall has over 30 years of executive and operational experience in strategic planning, vision development, long-range resource analysis, strategic forecasting, international operations and management, systems and operations analysis, systems engineering, warfare gaming and analysis, technology planning, and inspirational leadership under demanding conditions, including combat operations in the Vietnam War, the 1986 Libya "Line of Death" and strike operations, and the 1991 Gulf War.

He is the President and CEO of Strategic Synthesis, Ltd. (LLC), which he founded in June 1997. His naval service included three commands at sea, including the AEGIS Cruiser USS MOBILE BAY (CG 53), serving as the four-carrier 'Battle Force ZULU' Anti-Air Warfare Commander (AAWC) during the 1991 Gulf War in the Northern Arabian Gulf. Service ashore include duties in the Office of the Secretary of Defense, the Joint Staff, and the Office of the Chief of Naval Operations. He also served as Director of Professional Development at the U.S. Naval Academy.

In addition to his extensive experience in strategic planning and vision development, Dr. Woodall serves as a consulting senior systems engineer and systems analyst for a number of major defense and consulting firms. From May-December 2009, he was co-host of the radio program "Strategy with Passion" that aired on VoiceAmerica.com Business Channel. He is the author of the book *Strategic Forecasting in Long-Range Military Force Planning: With an Application to the Naval Case*, and is coauthor of the book *Strategy with Passion: A Leader's Guide to Exploiting the Future*.

In addition to his consulting work, Dr. Woodall is an active member of the Strike, Land Attack, and Air Defense (SLAAD) Division of the National Defense Industrial Association (NDIA), where he serves as Vice Chairman and as a member of the Executive Committee.

———

Printed in Great Britain
by Amazon